Understanding Service Oriented Architecture

Designing Adaptive Business Model for SMEs

by

DR. ASHISH SETH
DR. KIRTI SETH

FIRST EDITION 2020

Copyright © BPB Publications, India

ISBN: 978-93-88511-872

Distributors:

BPB PUBLICATIONS
20, Ansari Road, Darya Ganj
New Delhi-110002
Ph: 23254990/23254991

DECCAN AGENCIES
4-3-329, Bank Street,
Hyderabad-500195
Ph: 24756967/24756400

MICRO MEDIA
Shop No. 5, Mahendra Chambers,
150 DN Rd. Next to Capital Cinema,
V.T. (C.S.T.) Station, MUMBAI-400 001
Ph: 22078296/22078297

BPB BOOK CENTRE
376 Old Lajpat Rai Market,
Delhi-110006
Ph: 23861747

Published by Manish Jain for BPB Publications, 20 Ansari Road, Darya Ganj, New Delhi-110002 and Printed by him at Repro India Ltd, Mumbai

About the Author

Dr. Ashish Seth is an Author, Consultant, Researcher and Teacher. He is presently working as an Associate Professor in the Department of Computer Science & Engineering, INHA University Tashkent. He has more than 16 years of research and teaching experience. He worked at various universities in India and abroad at various academic positions and responsibilities. He is also serving as an editor, reviewer and evaluator for some reputed journals. His youtube channel provides educational video lectures on various areas of computer science. His online forum provides guidance to students on various subjects and helps them to discuss their problems. For his continuous dedication and contribution in enhancing the teaching learning process he has been awarded with Best Faculty award, Young Researcher award and Most Promising Educationist Award. He finds interest in reading and writing articles on emerging technologies.

Linkedin: https://www.linkedin.com/in/dr-ashish-seth-877b1116

Dr. Kirti Seth is presently working as an Associate Professor in School of Computer and Information Engineering, INHA University, Tashkent. She is PhD (Computer Science and Engineering) in the area of "Component Based Systems" from Department of Computer Sciences and Engineering, Dr. APJ Abdul Kalam Technical University, Lucknow (Uttar Pradesh), INDIA in 2016. M.Tech (Computer Science), from Banasthali Vidyapeeth, Banasthali, Rajasthan, INDIA, 2009. She also holds MSc (CS) degree and has been into research and academics for last fourteen years. She has published more than 40 research papers in reputed journals like ACM, Springer and Elsevier and authored four books. She is a member of Technical Review Committee for many reputed journals. She has been participating and organizing seminar, conferences, workshops, expert lecturers and technical events to share knowledge among academicians, researchers and to promote opportunities for new researchers. She has been awarded with Best Faculty award for her contribution in enhancing teaching learning activities.

Linkedin: https://in.linkedin.com/in/dr-kirti-seth-451b8699

Acknowledgements

This book is our voyage towards new knowledge and experiences. It has provided us the opportunity to present our abilities and motivation to conduct research and make recognized contributions to academia and industry. I owe our sincere thanks and appreciation to several people for their valuable contributions and suggestions to bring my work in present form.

Firstly, I thank the Almighty for blessing us with strength and patience to overcome all the hurdles which we faced during the course of this work.

We would like to pay gratitude to our parents (Sh. Harish Seth & Smt. Krishna Seth) and (Sh. Vinod Tyagi & Smt. Sushma Tyagi) for blessing and encouragement they have provided during every endeavor of our life. They are continuous source of support & motivation in all phases of our life.

We wish to express our deep sense of gratitude and everlasting indebtedness to Dr. Himanshu Aggarwal (Professor, Department of Computer Science & Engineering, Punjabi University, Patiala) whose advise, constant encouragement, invaluable suggestions and expert guidance were of at most help in completing this book .

I am grateful to Dr. Woo Sug Cho (First Vice Rector, Inha University in Tashkent, Uzbekistan) for his all-time support and motivation which paved us a way for successful completion of this book. We extend special thanks to him for giving us constant encouragement and directions from time to time. We are thankful to all our colleagues at INHA University for providing us valuable suggestions and advice which help a lot for bringing the improved quality in our work.

We would like to dedicate this work to our lovely twin daughters *Verda* and *Vindhya*, for being a *'Good Luck'* in our life. Finally, we wish to express our thanks to all our teachers, friends, relatives who helped directly or indirectly at different stages during the course of this work.

Ashish Seth
Kirti Seth

Preface

Evolution in technology is an ongoing process, the more the technology advances; the more is the thrust of making the things simpler. SOA is seen as a new type of architecture that defines how to defining interfaces so that service be used in context-free ways. SOA is more capable to handle the on demand requirements, further services in SOA be used in distributed fashion.

The content of this book is meant to enable enterprise system users to be able to process their daily business values chain activities through the proposed integrated model. The main focus of this book is to create business values chain integration model using service oriented methodology. The idea is on providing smooth integration of diverse systems and services that can help in making smooth business values chain activities which is needed in small and medium enterprises.

Service Oriented Architecture (SOA) has gained ground as a mechanism for defining business services and operating models. Thus, provides a structure for IT to deliver against the actual business requirements and adapt in a similar way to the business. Though SOA gives you the ability to more easily integrate IT systems, provide multi-channel access to your systems, and to automate business process, it is still not completely matured and adopted fully in the organization.

This book contains six chapters and the experiment covered in this book adopted a descriptive type of research in which data was collected from various sources and analyzed to come up with conclusion. Various statistical and soft computing techniques were used in this research at various phases to conclude results.

Chapter 1 titled "Service Oriented Architecture – an Introduction" outlines the contents of this book. This chapter starts with the introduction to the evolution of distributed technology, discusses the problem domains, understanding the SOA, its design and architecture, benefit and its role in organizations. It also covers the techniques used to do analysis, interpretation of data and result obtained in the experimental covered in the book.

Chapter 2 titled "Review of Service Oriented Systems" covers the thorough survey done on existing literature in the area of SOA, presents an overview of various aspects of this study through review. It is an attempt to fully understand the problem area and find the gap that exists in the area of research. An extensive survey of the existing research literature in the form of the research papers and articles published in different journals and magazines, conferences, text and reference books, and case studies has been done. It also focused on the review on the generic information of business values chain activities like ERP, CRM and SCM, focusing on their similarities and relationships. A brief summary of the research literature consulted for carrying out the research has also been presented.

Chapter 3 titled "Research Methodologies" covers in detail all the methods used in the research. It describes the way in which the present research work has been executed. The steps taken in preparation of respondent's database, scope of the study and questionnaire design have been explained. This chapter elaborates the method used to capture necessary research data, and what data should be collected. This involves testing of the validity and reliability of the questionnaire; it covers in details the different techniques used for evaluating of the proposed model. Techniques like GQM method, hypothesis method, fuzzy method, adaptive fuzzy method, fuzzy TOPSIS method and factor rating method are discussed in detail. It also focuses the status of present ERP system implemented in India and particularly discusses the approach of an Indian SMEs towards adopting SOA based systems.

Chapter 4 titled "Design and Implementation of a SOA Model – A Case Study "This chapter discusses the approach of SOA implementation and focus on identifying the factors of SOA systems. It explains the layered approach in details which is used to design the proposed model. This chapter further highlights the advantages of integrated model in comparison to traditional ERP. The chapter also highlights the system integration implementation environments, suggesting the software and hardware involved. It covers the unified modeling of the proposed model and present class diagrams for different business value chain activities.

Chapter 5 titled "Study of the inhibiting and success factors in SOA design and implementation" focuses on study of the critical success factors in SOA design and implementation. It covers aspects of SOA that need to be better understood in terms of their relevance to SOA evolution.

Chapter 6 titled "Testing of Service Based Model" covers an extensive discussion of the various methods used for evaluating different aspect of the proposed system. It discusses the results of the following experiments:

- Identification of implementation approaches.
- Reliability estimation of system using fuzzy approach.
- Reliability estimation of system using adaptive neuro-fuzzy approach.
- Evaluation of optimal service composition within a system using fuzzy TOPSIS.
- Evaluation of performance of proposed system using 'factor rating method'.
- Evaluation of proposed hypothesis using T-test.

The detailed analysis of experiments and result is presented in table forms as well as in graphical diagrams. The results captured from the survey questionnaire are analyzed and summary of the findings are also covered.

Thus, the scope of this book is to provide a reference model/ framework for an overall, integrated enterprise-wide SOA for SME to address business values chain activities in a holistic manner. The primary beneficiaries of this work would be the small and medium enterprises that are investing into the IT with an expectation of good results but within the constraints of limited budget.

We believe that experience documented in this book would be great help to understand the dimensions of this emerging technology and identify the research scope of service oriented development. It will be helpful for practitioners in collecting the data necessary for reliability prediction of SOA based model. Hence, this book could be referred to as an advance research for service-oriented integration oaf business value chained activities within an enterprise.

Regards

Ashish Seth
Kirti Seth

Errata

We take immense pride in our work at BPB Publications and follow best practices to ensure the accuracy of our content to provide with an indulging reading experience to our subscribers. Our readers are our mirrors, and we use their inputs to reflect and improve upon human errors if any, occurred during the publishing processes involved. To let us maintain the quality and help us reach out to any readers who might be having difficulties due to any unforeseen errors, please write to us at :

errata@bpbonline.com

Your support, suggestions and feedbacks are highly appreciated by the BPB Publications' Family.

Table of Contents

CHAPTER 1

Service Oriented Architecture – An Introduction

Structure

Objectives

After studying this chapter, one can able to:

- Understand the technology evolution in Information Systems.
- Understand SOA, its design, architecture, benefit, and its role in organizations.
- Understand the concept of SOA, its components and challenges.
- Understand techniques used to do analysis, interpretation of data and result obtained during the research.

Chapter Outline

This chapter outlines the concept of service-oriented architecture. It starts with the introduction to the evolution of distributed technology, discusses the problem domains, understanding the SOA, its design and architecture, benefit and its role in organizations. It also covers the techniques used to do analysis, interpretation of data, and result obtained during the research. Further, it elaborates the need of on-demand systems.

1.1 Introduction

With the advent of new technologies, enterprises are expecting more and more to keep pace with the growing challenges in the market. Business processes are expected to be smart enough to handle the on-demand business requirement. **Service Oriented Architecture (SOA)** is believed to provide a solution for today's business demand.

An SOA is a style of design that guides an organization during all aspect of creating and using business services including conception, modeling, design, development, deployment, management, versioning, and retirement. Though SOA gives an ability to more easily integrate IT systems, provide multi-channel access, and to automate business processes, it is still not matured and adopted fully in the organization. Researchers in this area comment that SOA adoption in India is facing a number of challenges to adopt it completely. Service oriented architecture helps to create business-driven development and provide solutions that truly meet needs of today's organizations and are readily adapted in future whenever there is a change the need.

1.2 Evolution of Distributed System Technologies

The software evolution has distinct phases or layers of growth; these layers are built up one by one over the last ten decades, with each layer come up with the improvement over the previous one and fulfilling the need of the time. Software evolution begins with the concept of 1 and 0 (i.e. bit) give rise to machine language, followed by assembly language, procedure-oriented, object-oriented, component-based to service-oriented (*Figure 1.1*).

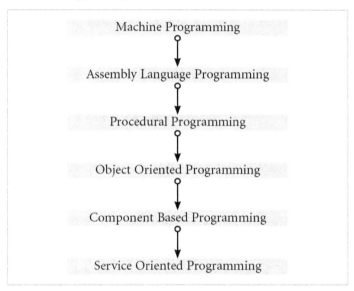

Figure 1.1   Technology Evolutions

Development in software technology continues to be dynamic. New tools and techniques are continuously announced in quick succession. This force the IT industry and players of this industry to look for new approaches to software design and development. These rapid advances appear to have created a situation of crisis within the industry. Right from the origin of programming languages and software development, we have seen a drastic evolution in software technology to meet the issues that arise due to technology crisis.

1.3 Getting Started with SOA

Transition often takes place in incremental steps; it does not require any organization to perform a complete overhaul of an IT infrastructure and development processes all at once. One can decide to rework an existing business process using an SOA or implement a new SOA application. Another organization may begin by adopting SOA based development methodologies and tools for a particular phase of the software development lifecycle.

An organization assures a reliable and flexible information flow between diverse applications and systems. As the organizations evolve, it begins to automate the orchestration of business and IT processes to align IT with the business goals and grow revenue while -containing costs.

1.3.1 Vision of SOA

The evolution of SOA is the same as we found in mid-1990 about Java. With the invention of Java, the programming approach has entered in the new paradigm. It was claimed (hyped) that Java is a panacea to all problems as it introduced a new concept of platform independency but as technology advances;

The more would be expected from it. In today's competitive scenario where business demand changes very frequently, the expectation from technology is raised to a level where we are expecting the business processes are developed in such a manner that they can adapt the frequent changes without affecting the overall organization business architecture. Thus, the need to assume business processes as a smart service that can be loosely coupled and form the basis of this work.

1.3.2 Role of SOA in organizations

SOA has gained ground as a mechanism for defining business services and operating models (For example, business-agile enterprise) and thus provide a structure for IT to deliver against the actual business requirements and adapt in a similar way to the business. The purpose of using SOA as a business mapping tool is to ensure that the services created clearly represent the business view and are not just what technologists think the business services should be.

At the heart of SOA, planning is the process of defining architectures for the use of information in support of the business, and the plan for implementing those architectures. Thus, SOA within the business is focused on a strict governance process and the use of semantics to improve the usefulness of services in business process innovation. SOA into a business can be think of as a set of layers, each of which has an objective to integrate business values chain activities and services to meet the business objective in a dynamic fashion as shown in *Figure 1.2* (Erl, 2004).

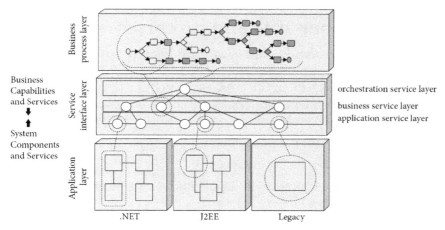

Figure 1.2   SOA Layers Focuses on Business Process and Services

1.3.3 SOA – Design Strategy and Architecture

Service-oriented architecture is a framework because every function and application appear on the network as a loosely coupled service. SOA is more than technology; it is also a design philosophy for reshaping business models and business processes. The adoption of open architectures and open standards is required to eliminate the integration barriers that exist today such as:

- Lack of open standards for connecting applications
- Cost of creating and maintaining customized formats
- Incompatibilities between disparate computing platforms
- Absence of trust definitions for secure communications
- Reliance on proprietary software from a single vendor

With SOA, integration is managed at the middleware level, not within each application, and the integration is addressed by a set of technical standards that form the basis for web services such as:

- **Web services definitions language (WSDL)** for discovery
- Internet protocols (e.g. TCP/IP) for transport

- **eXtensible mark-up language** (**XML**) for content formatting
- Messaging format (e.g., SOAP) for transmission
- **Business processing execution language** (**BPEL**) for process orchestration
- **Web security interoperability** (**WS-I**) for security

1.3.4 SOA benefits and promises

In later chapter, we will take a case study in which we will see how to design and implement a SOA based model; the case study will be an effort to propose an architecture on which the application can be built up of independent services, which have compatible interfaces. SOA promises such architecture to the IT world and provides:

- Rapid application development
- Automated business processes
- Multi-channel access to applications, including fixed and mobile devices

According to InfoWorld research report companies that have implemented SOA have experienced many benefits which can be seen in business and technology perspective are as follows:

Technology Perspective

- More flexible architecture
- Integration of existing applications
- Improved data integration
- Supports business process management
- Facilitates enterprise portal initiatives
- Speeds custom application development

Business Perspective

- More effective integration with business partners
- Support customer service initiatives
- Enable employee self-service
- Streamline the supply chain
- More effective use of external service providers

- Facilitate global sourcing

To summarize, service-oriented development provides the following benefits:

- **Reuse** – ability to create services that are reusable in multiple applications.

- **Efficiency** – new applications can be built easily using old and new services, focusing only on the data part rather than implementation issues.

- **Loose coupling technology** – the ability to model service independently without caring for the execution environment and to create messages that can be sent to any service.

- **Division of responsibility** – business issues must be handled by businesspeople, technology issues by technical people, and service contracts be defined to collaborate both groups.

Thus, the following factors that form the basis of motivation for an organization to adopt SOA:

- The need to respond quickly to on-demand change of business needs.

- The need to motivate reuse of technical assets across an enterprise.

These requirements form the basis to motivate migration to SOA, and require steps to optimize development and support costs, and call for the creation of standardized asset, that once created, may be run -anywhere.

1.3.5 SOA Challenges

The technology risk of SOA is particularly challenging due to the following factors:

- Early adoption and evolution of supporting technology

- Organization change is necessary since SOA crosses system -boundaries

- The architecture is enterprise in scope encompassing dispersed and heterogeneous systems

- The infrastructure is distributed requiring high availability and scalability

- The project life cycle methodology requires changes due to complex system dependencies, SOA specific design patterns, and the change impact on the infrastructure and users

- Program management is often complex due to the project scope, interdependencies, and new technology risks

- Quality assurance is difficult since services are distributed, have many interfaces, require new testing environments, and message-based testing tools

- New competencies must be developed spanning project management, analysis and design, development and operations

1.4 Scope of Service Based Systems in India

Enterprise systems such as **enterprise resource planning (ERP)**, **supply chain management (SCM)**, and **customer relationship management (CRM)** have been constructed as a critical success factor for any organizations to maintain their competitive advantage, but all these systems exist in isolation. Although there are number of independent intelligent solutions that exist in the market, though very efficient in its own but not good enough to improve the effective competitive advantage because each of the systems that exist in isolation and thus, lack of means for information sharing among each other. Further, many of the legacy systems were developed by using proprietary technologies and most of them are lack of standards like XML (Cruz et al., 2003). SOA is the need for current business. It has been seen increasing competitiveness of the business environment for a past decade.

Further, shortage of studies, research thrust and limited expertise in the area of SOA keep the application of SOA in small and medium enterprises limited. Also, in a country like India, whose major economy is dependent on the small and medium enterprises, the Indian government is promoting the growth in this sector. Successful examples of individual automated enterprise services and traditional ERP implementation systems exist, but there is a lack of holistic, integrated technical solutions that can be applied in small and medium-size enterprises.

Therefore, there is an immense need for a model that can specifically meet all the on-demand changing requirements of enterprises particularly for small and medium enterprises. After identifying the frequent changes in the business process, their impact, scope and hidden issues, it is possible to draw target enterprise SOA based architecture for SMEs. According to the literature available and the needs of the SMEs, the desired model should meet the following goals:

- It should consist of number of services, each capable of handling a single business task.

- Services must be loosely coupled, to minimize the dependency on others.

- It should use standard and open communication protocols.

- Implementation details should be separated from service -contracts / interfaces.

Keeping the above points in mind and existing research gaps, the need for such an SOA model is evident due to the numerous benefits it can bring to both small and medium-size enterprises.

Note

The researchers may use the following strategy to build any on-demand based adhoc system:

i. Investigate series of processes/activities (value chain activities) in **small and medium-size enterprises (SMEs)**

ii. Propose an SOA based design and implementation model for value chain activities (as identified in objective 1)

iii. Identify critical success factors for the proposed SOA model (risk analysis)

iv. Test and identify the inter-dependency of activities/processes within the proposed model

iv. Present use case diagram using unified modeling language (UML) for the proposed model

---

1.5 Research Methodology for SOA based systems

The research methodology refers to an action plan or framework that was adopted in carrying out any research. Based on literature survey and existing models, secondary data for research can be collected from related books, publication, annual reports, and records of organization under study. For the primary data, questionnaire cum personal interview method from randomly selected managers working at these selected organizations using SOA systems can be employed.

The questionnaire should be prepared based on your proposed model, and then the responses are taken from industry person to evaluate it. Data can be collected through questionnaire-cum-interview technique. The Questionnaire is pre-tested on some of the managers, and thus pre-tested questionnaire is administered to all the sampled respondents. Appropriate statistical techniques and MATLAB tools can be used for collection, analysis and interpretation of the sample data. The activities include in accomplishing this task is described in following steps: (*Figure 1.3*)

- Study of the selected organizations particularly small and medium enterprises.
- Preparation of the database of the respondents.
- Formulization of the questionnaire through consultation, feedback, and survey.
- Testing of the questionnaire.
- Mapping of the questionnaire to the research objectives.
- Analyzing the collected data and drawing valid conclusions regarding the objectives of study, with the application of various statistical tools.
- Design and implement the proposed model for current research work using layered architecture.
- Identify the critical success factors.
- Evaluating the proposed model using different statistical and a neuro-computing technique, that include t-test, fuzzy, adaptive neuro-fuzzy, and factor rating methods.
- Preparing use case diagram using unified modeling language for the proposed model.

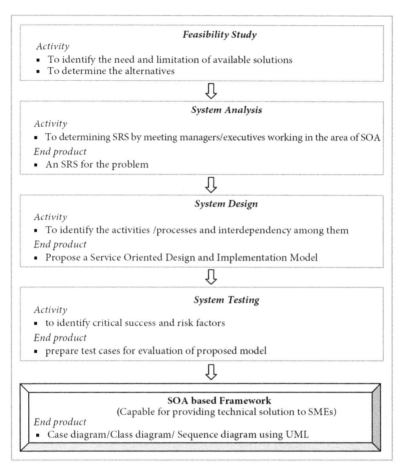

*Figure 1.3 Graphical Representation of
steps needed to design SOA Framework*

1.6 Summary

Evolution in technology is an ongoing process, the more the technology advances; the more is the thrust of making the things simple. SOA can be seen as a new type of architecture that defines how to define interfaces so that service is used in context-free ways. SOA is more capable of handling the on-demand requirements; further services in SOA be used in a distributed fashion.

This chapter has outlined the basic structure of the book which covers the introductions of the work, need of the study, objectives defined for this work and finally covers the organization of chapters in book (i.e. summarizes the contents of each chapter). The objective of this book is to enable enterprise system users to be able to process their daily business values chain activities through the proposed integrated model.

The main focus is to create business values chain integration model using service-oriented methodology. The idea is on providing a smooth integration of diverse systems and services that can help in making smooth business values chain activities which are needed in small and medium enterprises. Thus, the scope of this book is to provide a reference model/framework for an overall, integrated enterprise-wide SOA for SME to address business values chain activities in a holistically. The primary beneficiaries of this book would be students, researchers, consultants, and IT managers associated with the small and medium enterprises that are investing into the IT with an expectation of good results but within the constraints of a limited budget.

Questions

Q1. What do you understand by the term *ad-hoc* requirements?

Q2. Comment on the need for Service based Systems in a country like India?

Q3. Identify the benefits of SOA based systems for small and medium enterprises.

Q4. Do a short survey to identify the risk and challenges to start a new company.

Key Terms

SOA Service Oriented Architecture

B2B Business to business

BPM Business Process Management

CSS Customer Services and Support

SME Small and Medium Enterprises

WSDL Web Services Definitions Language

XML eXtensible Mark-up Language

SOAP Simple Object Access Protocol

BPEL　Business Processing Execution Language

WS-I　Web Security Interoperability

References

- Kostas K., Grace A. L., Dennis B., Smith M. L. (2007). "The Landscape of Service-Oriented Systems: A Research Perspective". *International workshop on Systems Development in SOA Environments*, SDSOA '07: ICSE Workshops. Vol. 12, No. 3, pp 345–359.

- Mike P., Willem J., Heuvel V. (2007). "Service Oriented Architectures: Approaches, Technologies and Research Issues". *The International Journal on Very Large Data Bases*, Springer-Verlag New York, Inc. Secaucus, NJ, USA, Vol. 16, No. 3, pp 389–415.

- Sriram A, Srinivas P., Jai G. (2005). "Perspectives on Service Oriented Architecture in Services Computing". *IEEE International Conference*, Vol. 2, No. 1, pp 228–243.

- Cruz I.F., Rajendran, A. (2003). "Semantic Data Integration in Hierarchical Domains". *IEEE Intelligent Systems*.Vol.2, No. 2, pp 66–73.

- Zadeh L.A. (1975). "The Concept of a Linguistic Variable and its Application Approximate Reasoning", *Part 1, 2, and Part 3, Information Sciences*, Vol. 8, No. 3, 199–249; Vol. 8, No. 4, 301–357; Vol. 9, No. 1, 43–58.

CHAPTER 2

Review of Service Oriented Systems

Structure

Objectives

After studying this chapter, one can be able to:

- Understand the extent to which SOA has been adopted in organization
- Understand enterprise resource planning in context of SOA implementation
- Understand customer relationship management in context of SOA implementation
- Understand supply chain management in context of SOA implementation

Chapter Outline

This chapter covers the thorough survey done on existing literature in the area of SOA. It also covers review on the generic information of business values chain activities like ERP, CRM and SCM, focusing on their similarities and relationships.

2.1 Introduction

The objective of this chapter is to study existing design and implementation models to identify the gaps. SOA systems are large, complex and unfamiliar for the organizations to be implemented. There are very few conventional models have been proposed by some researchers working in SOA system. The literature survey and analysis suggest that very few among the existing model is complete in design and implementation of SOA systems particularly for small and medium level organizations. The conventional model fails to cope well with the need for the mutual fit between the enterprise resource package and the organization.

2.2 Impact of Service Oriented System – Survey

In the early years of computing, we had only monolithic applications running on stand-alone machines. From the era of monolithic systems of early '60s, we have seen the development of structured, object based, client/server, 3-tier, N-tier, distributed systems, component-based systems and finally the service-oriented architectures of the modern age (*Figure 2.1*).

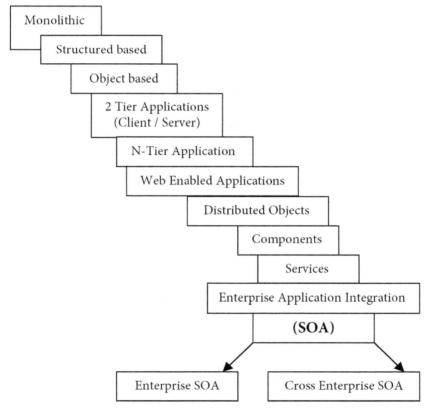

Figure 2.1   SOA Evolution

Service Oriented Architecture (SOA) is a computer system's architectural style for creating and using business processes, throughout their lifecycle. SOA allows exchange of data between applications and become a part of business process. The market for *core* service-oriented architecture technology reached $50 billion by 2014 (*www.searchwebservices.com*). According to WinterGreen Research, SOA markets at $470 million in 2008 reached to $18.4 billion by 2014.

This growth is expected because SOA enables the flexible IT architecture and adhoc on demand features that is needed to respond to market shifts brought by speeded product cycles and competitive challenges. *Table 2.1* shows some companies which are profiled for SOA and technology-based development.

According to Gartner estimates, by 2013, at least 70% of large enterprises have more than 35% of their application portfolios based on SOA, up from fewer than 5% of organizations in 2008. Another report from Springboard Research estimates that the SOA market in India would have grown at a **compound annual growth rate (*CAGR*)** of 49% from 2008-20010, making it one of the fastest growing markets in the **Asia-Pacific (APAC)** region.

Table 2.1   Companies Profiled with their Product for Technology Based Development

IBM	I2
Microsoft	Infravio
Oracle	Inovis
SAP	Interwoven
BEA	IONA
Sun Microsystems	Item Field
Amber Point	Kabria
Attachmate WRQ	MQ Software
BMC Software	OpenText
Cape Clear	Pegasystems
CAPE Systems	Progress Software
EMC Documentum	Savvion
Envoy Technologies	SOA Software
FileNet	Sybase
Fiorano	Synergy Financial Systems
Fujitsu	Tibco
Go Ahead	Vitria
GXS	webMethods
HP	Zebra Technologies

According to a report dated Aug 2009 by Frost and Sullivan, the SOA market in India till 2009 was at a nascent stage and it largely remains untapped by major vendors although numerous opportunities exist. Dhruv Singhal (2009), Senior Director – Fusion Middleware Sales Consulting, Oracle India, pointed out, *Today, the primary driver for SOA adoption is the business demand that forces enterprise data centers to deliver more with minimal resources. SOA adopts open standards to reduce integration costs, provide composite applications, and reduce custom coding through configuration and enable self-sufficiency for the end user. It is expected to be a critical business enabler rather than a mere IT tool.*

IBM is the defacto industry standard market leader in SOA. IBM dominates SOA with 64% of the market; the rest of market is divided between 12 other participants with measurable market share, none of whom have even been able to garner as much as 8% of the market. IBM stands alone as the leader in SOA, inventing the concept of refining reusable solutions that have been around for a long time, while the IBM SOA can be a solution to be used on a global business works; the SOA services as a middleware infrastructure are implemented flexible enough to give to local differences. Forrester surveyed that Sixty-eight percent of enterprises say they are using SOA or will be using it by the end of 2020. Fifty-six percent are using SOA now, and that number jumps to 74 percent when considering only Global 2000 organizations. *Table 2.2* below shows current statistics by research agencies reflecting the current trends in SOA adaptation.

Table 2.2 Statistics by Research Agencies Showing Current Trends in SOA Adaptation

Companies Perspective
• **15%** of small companies (with fewer than 100 employees) have SOA efforts underway, compared to 35% of companies with more than 500 employees. (Nucleus Research)
• **12%** — that's the average growth rate of companies with *well-aligned IT-business operations*, versus 4% overall. (BTM Institute)
• **40%** of companies with SOA spend between 10 and 30 percent of their overall IT budgets on SOA projects. Most have increased their SOA budgets over last year. (IBM)
• **37%** of companies implementing SOA report seeing positive return on investment from SOA — which, by the way, isn't too shabby (Nucleus Research)
• **29%** of companies with advanced SOA deployments are using SOA governance software, compared of 17% of companies still in earlier stages of SOA. (Aberdeen)
• **25%** of mainframe companies have SOA efforts now in progress and another one-third are planning or considering SOA. At least half say they are or will employ mainframes in a central role in SOA. (Unisphere Research/SHARE)
• **50%** of new mission-critical operational applications and business processes were designed around SOA, a number will jump to more than 80 percent by next few years. (Gartner)

Developers Perspective
• **49%** of developers working with SOA say they can now complete a typical SOA project within three months – more than twice as many as a year ago. Plus, more than 60% of all SOA projects are now developed and deployed within just six months. (Evans Data)
• **61%** of advanced SOA deployers saw a reduction in the number of software defects discovered in production, compared to 18% of non--deploying companies could say they were able to reduce defects. (-Aberdeen)
• **61%** of advanced SOA deployers saw a reduction in the number of software defects discovered in production, compared to 18% of non--deploying companies could say they were able to reduce defects. (-Aberdeen)
• **75%** of mainframe developers said they want to modernize their -systems. But 52%, also said they had concerns about their system's ability to actually support SOA. (Software AG)
• **24%** of developers said that they've used SOA techniques, up 85% from the previous year. (Evans Data)
Higher Management Perspective
• **48%** of CIOs are planned to open their SOAs *to the cloud* in 2014 — the cloud being *where their current and potential trading partners are.* (McKinsey)

Small and Medium Enterprises (**SME**) cannot apply the higher levels of **Capability Maturity Model** (**CMM**) and to define precisely its business processes, as SME cannot have enough data and experience. Moreover, they are restricted to their budget for investment in technology, and therefore have a limited possibility to design stable business processes. Hence they have specific requirements on the software systems they use (Manuela M. et al., 2009).

Therefore, any software system for SME must be able to adapt itself dynamically to changing business conditions. A use of modern software systems depends on the skills and knowledge of (end) users of the systems. Properly used SOA can substantially enable new business turns, and has many technical advantages. The model proposed in this work is especially preferable for small-to-medium enterprises, but it can also be applied in large enterprises for different reasons. The kernel of the solution is based on the SOA-based generalization of the concept of usability and on a technical turn enabling agility of business processes.

 The architecture of SOA-based applications is different from traditional software architecture where the architecture is mainly static. The SOA-based application architecture is dynamic, i.e., the application may be composed at runtime using existing services. Thus, SOA has provided a new direction for software architecture study, where the architecture is determined at runtime and architecture can be dynamically changed at runtime to meet the new software requirements.

2.2.1 Review of existing work in SOA based systems

In order to design service oriented architecture there is an immense need to know the scope and size of the work involved. For this purpose, detailed review needs to be done. Existing work on SOA based system is summarized in the form of the following *Table 2.3.*

Table 2.3   Review of Existing Work in SOA based Systems

S.No.	Citation	Major Work
1	Xing S. et al. (2013)	Authors claimed that the in SOA, service consumers and providers need to evaluate the trust levels of potential partners before engaging in interactions. They presented trust model, called the priority-based trust model that drives the trustworthiness of a service provider from its historical performance and designated referees. They claimed that there model has betters performance in dynamic environments.
2	Fatima B. et al. (2012)	Authored proposed a solution to overcome several obstacles that force the installation of the SOA within the company. Paper described an extended service-oriented architecture – SOAda for supporting a decision aspect. Authors presented mete-model **Model decisional of service (MDS)** to define a new set of concepts necessary for modeling the three sights.

S.No.	Citation	Major Work
3	Zhang M.W. et al. (2011)	Proposed a novel service composition approach based on production QoS rules. Authors adopted *black-box* analysis method of optimizing composite services, in their approach, the execution information of the composite service is recorded into a log first, which will be taken as the basis of the subsequent statistical analysis and data mining. Then, the timely QoS values of the Web services are estimated and the production QoS rules being used to qualitatively express the different performances of the Web service QoS in different environments are mined. They employed the mined QoS knowledge of the Web services to optimize the composite service selection.
4	Jacqui C. et al. (2010)	Paper proposed an information security framework for SOA, authors suggested SOA security components for a service-oriented environment. Components can be developed collectively from service oriented architecture design principles, the ISO/IEC 27002:2005 standard, and other service-oriented architecture governance frameworks. Proposed security framework claimed to assist organizations in determining information security controls for service-oriented architectures.
5	Joyce E. H. (2010)	The author suggested the method of web service selection by meeting the user's requirements, expressed as weights over QoS criteria. Paper addressed the issue of selecting and composing Web services not only according to their functional requirements but also to their transactional properties and QoS characteristics.

S.No.	Citation	Major Work
6	Granebring A. et al. (2009)	Researchers explained why **service-oriented business intelligence** (**SOBI**) required in new development and how to make a strategy to introduce daily decision support in the retail trade. There work answered the question: like how to draft a BI strategy for all parts of the retail enterprise? By excellent data warehouse quality; choosing an area for common decision support; starting simply, with metrics (sale, gross margin, number of customers) to get users started and then continue the iterative process of practicing more comparing and personalized BI. In essence, services act as layer of abstraction between the business and the technology.
7	Nirmal K. et al (2009)	In this paper authors argued that in the basic SOA model, access to metadata is too static and results in inflexible interactions between requesters and providers. Authors propose specific extensions to the SOA model to allow service providers and requestors to dynamically expose and negotiate their public behavior, resulting in the ability to specialize and optimize the middleware supporting an interaction. They introduced a middleware architecture supporting this extended SOA functionality, and describe a conformant implementation based on standard web services middleware. Finally, demonstrates the advantages of their approach with a detailed real-world scenario.

S.No.	Citation	Major Work
8	Stuart K. et al. (2009)	Article dealt with the aspects of governance, give some insight into the importance of governance in the context of enterprise SOA and a vendor organization. General issues of product governance are explored, and the impact of service-orientation will have on the vendor organization is discussed. Paper highlighted the similarities and differences between IT governance, product portfolio governance and introduce new governance areas for the vendor company.
9	Francis G.M. (2009)	Author specified the OASIS reference architecture for service oriented architecture. It follows from the concepts and relationships defined in the OASIS reference model for service oriented architecture. While it remains abstract in nature, their work describes one possible template upon which a SOA concrete architecture can be built.
10	Navabpour S. et al. (2008)	Authors described the implementation of a mash up that integrates travel services. Constructed the service wrappers for various travel services. Given a travel request from end user, the proposed system can decompose the user query into sub queries and send those sub queries to primitive services in order to find the best way of traveling. The shortest path algorithm is used to find the cheapest price via the combination of flight, train, and bus.

S.No.	Citation	Major Work
11	Liam O.B. et al. (2008)	In this paper authors outlined some of the major aspects of SOA introduction and focus on performance and QoS which are major pieces to get right if the SOA implementation is to be successful. Author suggested that when an organization wants to introduce the use of SOA there are some aspects that it needs to consider that include: • The identification and mining of services from its existing/legacy systems • The integration of common/shared services provided by one government agency and used by other agencies services with existing/legacy systems • The acquisition and development of an SOA infrastructure (including middleware) • The development of services and development of applications from services
12	Apostolos M. et al. (2008)	Presented the design of an enterprise-based architecture. The proposed architecture is compliant with established practices in the building automation field and focuses on catering for a wide spectrum of building and enterprise level services. The architectural framework proposed assembles all underlying functionality and hides complexity from the upper-layer applications.

S.No.	Citation	Major Work
13	Fischer T. et al. (2008)	Authors discussed the problems arising from the requirement of runtime adaptation and presented solution by replacing service implementations at execution time in a service-oriented component model. This paper presented an approach to replace service implementations at runtime to provide a foundation for autonomic, self--managing, self-healing, self-optimizing, self-configuring and self-adaptive applications.
14	Wang J. et al. (2008)	The author proposed the SOA based decision support system for oil production. Paper claims many advantages, such as easy integration, good maintainability. Authors claimed that the research makes the best of all the resource of the oil industry, and makes great integration of all the information system. It has a great effect on the upgrading and transformation of ERP.
15	Jianqiang H. et al. (2008)	Elaborates that enterprises service bus as key status in SOA based enterprise integration application environment. It is responsible for wrapping legacy application to service, synchronous or asynchronous transport, and supporting the enterprise business integration across different organizations. Major contribution of paper was to present unified transport adaptation and service adaptation to improve the interoperability of enterprise applications across different organizations; author also defined multiple SOAP scheduling algorithm and SOAP security framework for B2B integration and ecommerce development.

S.No.	Citation	Major Work
16	Luciano R. et al. (2007)	Authors argued that, to handle different forms of data poses a big challenge for application developers, and the challenge increases in size when there is broad diversity of programming models in use. He provided the solutions that are composed of services that offer business functionality as a unit or as a whole. These services will access data from different data source types and potentially need to aggregate data from different data source types with different data formats.
17	Kostas K. et al. (2007)	The paper attempted to investigate an initial classification of challenge areas related to service orientation and service-oriented systems. Paper outlined a set of emerging opportunities to be used. From a business perspective, service-oriented systems are a way of exposing legacy functionality to remote clients; authors suggested that SOA serve as bridging the gap between business models and software infrastructure and flexibly supporting changing business needs.

S.No.	Citation	Major Work
18	Mike P. (2007)	This paper reviewed technologies and approaches that unify the principles and concepts of SOA with those of event-based programming. The paper focused on the ESB and describes a range of functions that are designed to offer a manageable, standards- based SOA backbone that extends middleware functionality throughout by connecting heterogeneous components and systems and offers integration services. Paper proposed an approach to extend the conventional SOA to cater for essential ESB requirements that include capabilities such as service orchestration, *intelligent* routing, provisioning, integrity and security of message as well as service management.
19	Sriram A. et al. (2007)	This paper focused on providing an overview of service oriented architecture with emphasis on the evolution of SOA from other technologies such as object oriented programming and distributed computing. Subsequently, this work delves into exploring SOA from multiple perspectives, such as the relevance of SOA in EAI, SOA features of J2EE and .NET.
20	Boris S. et al. (2006)	This paper suggested improvements with respect to the business-application alignment in the design of application software. Authors proposed a model-driven service-oriented approach which is essentially concerned with consistency as the target quality to ensure business-application alignment; they have shown how different business and application models.

S.No.	Citation	Major Work
21	Amelia M. et al. (2006)	The paper seeked to review the factors and methods used to integrate multiple ERP systems in an EAI environment. Author also argued that companies continue to realize that an EAI system is necessary to comply with SOA, more information and requests are voiced to help with enhancing the systems and business portion for the auditor of a data warehouse system.
22	Yan Z. (2006)	This paper provided insight and discussion regarding to what SOA is, what it really means to an enterprise, where it is right now, where it is leading to, how to practice it, the expected benefits, and how to calculate associated ROI. It includes discussions on SOA concepts, technologies, and best practices based on practice experience, survey from public sources, as well as initial ideas and contributions. Author proposed a practical modeling approach for **enterprise architecture (EA)** development that can help to bridge EA with solution architecture.
23	Lorenzoli D. et al. (2006)	This paper proposed an approach to design self-adaptive applications, which can react to changes in the implementation of services, thus avoiding unexpected failures. The architecture proposed in this paper automatically detects possible integration mismatches, and dynamically executes suitable adaptation strategies. The paper presented an application, the personal mobility manager, which integrates heterogeneous web services, identifies failures that derive from dynamic changes in the integrated services, and illustrates the self--adaptive design solution which can prevent run time failures.

S.No.	Citation	Major Work
24	Zimmer-mann O. et al. (2005)	This paper discussed the rationale behind the decision for SOA, process choreography, and web services, suggests combination of business dynamics and domain-specific functional characteristics creates many challenges for IT. Authors identified that an SOA-based approach with process choreography is perfectly valid for the order entry management scenario and it must also considered for other technical benefits included separation of concerns through strict layering, improved resource management via compensation and runtime reuse of shared application functionality made available as business and application services.
25	Fumiko S. et al. (2005)	Authors argued that the **service component architecture (SCA)** is an emerging technology as a standardized programming model for SOA applications, and therefore the SCA policy framework has also been discussed in the research community. This work offered value-added SCA policy tools for easy development of SOA application. There are many pattern-based approaches for nonfunctional requirements.
26	Bieberstein N. et al. (2005)	Proposed methodology for service architectures which focus on service discovery and suggest notation for the service architecture. Proposed methodology focused on the earliest activities of SOA development.

S.No.	Citation	Major Work
27	Ali A. et al. (2005)	Authors proposed a **service-oriented modeling architecture (SOMA)**, which provides modeling, analysis, design techniques, and activities to define the foundations of a SOA. Model can be useful for defining the elements in each of the SOA layers and making critical architectural decisions at each level up to some extent.
28	Zimmermann (2004)	In his work he discussed the case of SOAD **Service-oriented analysis and design (SOAD)**: which reinforces well-established, general software architecture principles such as information hiding, modularization, service choreography, service repositories, This methodology included portions of **business process modeling (BPM)** and **object-oriented analysis and design (OOAD)**, addresses the divide between WS-BPEL and WSDL.
29	Mark E. (2004)	His work started with business decomposition, which identifies business use cases and processes. The business use cases are then used to identify services. His work aimed to identify business components, and the methods to analyze processes within the subsystems.
30	Zimmermann et al. (2004)	His work focused on modeling the business' services as well as linking business processes to services. His finding was to identify the agile methods as applied to SOA.

2.2.2 Review of existing work in evaluating SOA based system

Most organizations that want to build service oriented architecture don't have a clue about how to approach the cost estimate. Literature on SOA reveals that to calculate the cost of an SOA has been a challenge. SOA can't cost out like a construction project where every resource required is tangible and is easily accountable for calculating the total project costly. Since to compute the cost of many notions like: understanding domain in proper context, understanding how much required resources cost, understanding how the work will get done and analyzing what can go wrong are some of intangible resources that are always required and are difficult to measure. According to Linthicum D. (2007), the risk and impact of SOA are distributed and pervasive across applications, therefore, it is critical to perform an architecture evaluation early in the software life cycle.

In computer science we have many established testing methods and tools to evaluate the software systems but unfortunately they do not work well for systems that are made up of services. Through wide literature survey, the existing various testing tools and evaluation methods for evaluating service based applications is summarized along with their limitation in a *Table 2.4*.

Table 2.4 Summary of different SOA based project evaluation approaches with their limitations

S.No.	Approach	Description	Limitations
1	COCOMO II related approaches	COCOMOII considers two types of reused components, namely black-box components and white-box components.	• COCOMOII is generally inadequate to accommodate the cost estimation needs for SOA-based s/w development. • COCOMO II model by itself is inadequate to estimate effort required when reusing service-oriented resources.
2	IFPUG	It provides simple range matrices for software cost -evaluation.	Its measures leads to *same quantities* for *different* software units.

S.No.	Approach	Description	Limitations
3	COSMIC	This model provides open range scales to take into account possibly high complexity functions.	Wider set of guidelines for practical application of COSMIC measurement would still has to test and experience.
4	Dave Linthicum formula	cost of SOA = (cost of data complexity + cost of service complexity + cost of process complexity + enabling technology -solution)	• The other aspects of the calculation is suggested to follow similar means without clarifying essential -matters • This approach is not a real metric • 10 to 20 percent variations in cost are expected
5	Function point analysis and software sizing	Source line of code and function point are the two predominant sizing measures. Function point measures software system size through quantifying the amount of functionality provided to the user in terms of the number of inputs, outputs, inquires, and files.	• Effort of wrapping legacy code and data to work, as services cannot be assigned to any functional size. • There are lacks of guidelines for practical application of COSMIC measurement in SOA context.

S.No.	Approach	Description	Limitations
6	Liu service points method	Software size estimation is based on the sum of the sizes of each service. i.e *Size = (n,i) (Pi * P)* where *Pi* is an infrastructure factor with empirical value, is related to the supporting infrastructure, technology and governance -processes.	The calculation of P for various services is not discussed in detail. *(P* represents a single specific service's estimated size that varies with different service types)
7	SMAT-AUS framework	Generic SOA application could be sophisticated and comprise a combination of project types, breaking the problem into more manageable pieces.	Specify how all of pieces are estimated and the procedure required for practical estimation of software development cost for SOA-based systems is still being developed.
8	SMART	Can be adopted for service mining cost estimation.	Currently there are no other metrics suitable for the different projects beneath the SMAT-AUS framework.
9	GQM	Based on the assumption that SOA follows different goals on different levels of EA abstraction.	Identification of relevant project types and context factors are not clear.

S.No.	Approach	Description	Limitations
10	Divide-and-Conquer approach	It recursively decompose the problem into smaller sub problems until all the sub-problems are sufficiently simple enough, and then to solve the sub-problems. Resulting solutions are then recomposed to form an overall solution.	Service classification can be different for different purposes, there is not a standard way to categorize services and method does not focus on this issue. • Approach mainly concentrating on cost estimation for service integration.
11	Work Breakdown Structure approach	Based on the principle of divide and conquer theory, this framework. could satisfy different requirements of SOA-based s/w cost estimation.	What will be the metric of different types is not properly explained.

2.2.3 Review of Existing Work in Estimating Reliability of SOA Based Systems

Reliability is one of the most important non-functional requirements for software. Accurately estimating reliability for **service oriented systems (SOS)** is not an easy task, and many researchers have proposed different approaches to SOS reliability estimation (Tyagi K. et al., 2012). IEEE 610.12-1990 defines reliability as *the ability of a system or component to perform its required functions under stated conditions for a specified period of time*. The primary objective of reliability is to guarantee that the resources managed and used by the system are under control. It also guarantees that a user can complete its task with a certain probability when it is invoked. Software reliability management is defined in IEEE 982.1-1988 as *The process of optimizing the reliability of software through a program that emphasizes software error prevention, fault detection and removal, and use of measurements to maximize reliability in light of project constraints such as resources, schedule, and performance.* Thus, any reliable system is one that must guarantee and take care of fault prevention, fault tolerance, fault removal, and fault forecasting.

So far, most of the research on software reliability engineering focuses on system testing and system-level reliability growth models. Approach for the reliability analysis of evolving software systems is well-illustrated in work of Musa et al. (2004). However, SOA is not taken into account in any of these approaches, but Goseva P. et al. (2001) and Gokhale et al. (2007), did remarkable work for architecture-based empirical software reliability analysis in relation to architecture-based empirical software reliability analyses. Although the reliability of SOA systems cannot be completely estimated, we can estimate the reliability to a larger extent by analyzing the SOA characteristics and identifying the corresponding requirements. Thorough study has been done to identify the characteristics and define a corresponding requirement. Significant work done in the direction of reliability estimation of SOA is summarized in *Table 2.5*.

Table 2.5 Summary of Existing Work in SOA Reliability

S. No	Model Name	Proposer	Findings
1	ReServE	Danilecki A. et al. (2011)	• A model ensured that business processes are consistently perceived by client and services. • It transparently recovers the state of a business process, when a service fails, its **service proxy unit** (**SPU**) can initiate the rollback-recovery process.

S. No	Model Name	Proposer	Findings
2	Component Model	Singh et al. (2011)	• Proposed to transform annotated UML component models into a bayesian model. • Can be used for reliability prediction during the design phase.
3	Analyzed SHARPE	Gokhale, et al (2007)	• For estimating component failure rates. It was found that the system reliability could be increased, if the fault density per component was reduced.
4	Analyzed-stock market system	Wang et al. (2006)	• Mapped to component failure probabilities. • Predict the system reliability. • Derived transition probabilities from recorded transitions between components.
5	Unified Reliability Modeling Framework	Grassi V. (2005)	• Automatic and compositional reliability prediction method. • Provides a hierarchical reliability model.

S. No	Model Name	Proposer	Findings
6	Service-Oriented Software Reliability Model (SORM).	Tsai et al. (2004)	It tried to determine the reliability of each component and their -relationship. It consists of two stages: • Group testing to evaluate the reliability of atomic services; and evaluation of composite services through the analysis of components and their relationships.

2.3 Understanding enterprise resource planning system – SOA Context

Enterprise resource planning (ERP) is business management software that allows an organization to use a system of integrated applications to manage the business. Similar definitions by other people are as follows:

- ERP systems are *"comprehensive, packaged software solution that seeks to integrate the complete range of a business' processes and functions in order to present a holistic view of the business from a single information and IT architecture"* (Gable 1998).

- ERP differs from earlier information systems in its capacity to disseminate information in real-time and increase organizational flexibility and agility (Markus et al., 2000).

- ERP provides the organization windows of opportunity for strategic changes. (anonymous)

However, due to the integration of large scale, ERP implementation is a complex and highly inter-dependent task (Sharma et al., 2003). According to the survey conducted by Deloitte, the rate of on-time and within budget ERP implementation is less than 20%. Also, the possible conflicts between the existing organizational culture and the culture assumption embedded in the ERP system escalates the difficulties of ERP implementation and makes ERP project prone to fail.

2.3.1 ERP Vendors

Large Enterprise ERP (ERP Tier I)

The ERP market for large enterprises is dominated by three companies: SAP, Oracle, and Microsoft. (*source*: EnterpriseAppsToday; enterprise ERP buyer's guide: SAP, Oracle, and Microsoft)

Midmarket ERP (ERP Tier II)

For the midmarket, vendors include Infor, QAD, Lawson, Epicor, Sage and IFS. (*source*: EnterpriseAppsToday; Midmarket ERP Buyer's Guide)

2.3.2 Objectives of an ERP

ERP is available for a wide range of industries, including financial services companies and companies focused on customer service. According to Jie M.W. (2007) the common objectives of ERP include:

- Repeatable processes
- Lower training costs
- Reduced inventory costs
- Improved business visibility
- Increased profits

2.3.3 Enterprise Resource Planning Modules

ERP system architecture is *modular* in form and dynamic in nature, which provides easy expansion and scalability for itself to be modified (Bakry & Bakry, 2005). From operational perspective, modules of an ERP are working as an integrated information system and deliver a single database. An ERP system has common functional areas; these are called and grouped together as *ERP modules*. The general modules of ERP are depicted in *Figure 2.2* are as follows: (*source: www.open-source-erp-site.com*)

- Financial
- Management accounting
- Human resources
- Manufacturing

- Sales and Distribution
- Project management

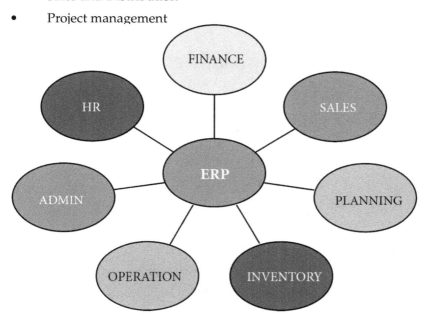

Figure 2.2   General Modules of an ERP

2.4 Understanding customer relationship management – SOA Context

CRM is about handling customer related services using technology to organize, automate, and synchronize customer services and technical support. **Customer relationship management** (**CRM**) is about relationship management in the context of software solutions. It may exist between companies and their vendors, companies and their customers, vendors and their suppliers, employees, different departments of the same company, and so on. At the core CRM business processes support the basic steps of customer life cycle, which includes attracting to present and acquiring the new customers, serving the customers and finally, retaining the customers.

2.4.1 CRM Vendors

Currently, there are mainly four market leaders within the CRM landscape they are SAP, Microsoft, Oracle, and Salesforce.com (AMR research, 2013). Good CRM help the business process to optimize customer life cycle management and improve relationship between customer and the company.

2.4.2 CRM Objectives

Primary objectives of CRM in the business strategy are as follows:

- To discover new customers and increase customer revenue
- To simplify marketing and sales process
- To cross sell products more effectively
- To make call centers more efficient
- To provide better customer service

Benefits: The following are the benefits of CRM processes:

- Collect customer related data
- Develop better communication channels
- Create detailed profiles of individual customers
- Reduced costs of buying and using product and services
- Identify new selling opportunities
- Increased market share and profit margin
- Enhanced customer loyalty
- Increased revenues
- More effective reach and marketing
- Improved customer service and support
- Improved response time to customer requests for information
- Improved quality communication and networking
- Increased customer satisfaction
- Better stand against global competition
- Improved ability to meet customer requirements
- Access to customer account history, order information, and customer information at all touch points

2.4.3 CRM Modules

CRM concerns about analytic, and collaborative perspective on the relationship between customers and the company. The modules are as follows:

- Sales functions
- Supplier relationship management
- Reports and dashboards statistics
- Marketing functions
- Customer service
- Automatization at workflows

2.5 Understanding supply chain management – SOA Context

Supply chain management (**SCM**) is the monitoring of materials, information, and finances as they move in a process from supplier to manufacturer to wholesaler to retailer and finally to consumer. Supply chain management involves coordinating and integrating these flows both within and among companies. SCM model primarily focuses on five processes as shown in *figure 2.3*. (*source: www.cgnglobal.com*)

- Plan
- Source
- Make
- Deliver
- Return

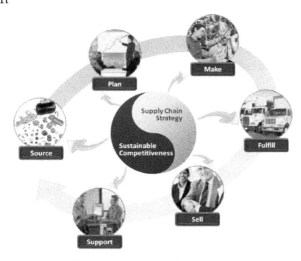

Figure 2.3   SCM Processes

SCM vendors

According to Gartner reports, the major SCM vendors are SAP, Oracle, JDA Software. SAP held the top spot with 22.4 percent of SCM software revenue and Oracle is the only other vendor to have double-digital market share.

SCM Modules

Common SCM modules in the marketplace includes inventory, order management, purchasing, e-procurement, cost management, services procurement, strategic sourcing, demand planning, supply planning, and so on. In general customers, company, design partners, material suppliers, contract manufacturers, logistic providers are considered as stake holder of SCM. Following are the advantage of SCM particularly for small companies:

- Increased efficiency
- Reduced costs
- Increased output
- Increased profits

2.5.1 Integration and interoperability among business values chain activities

Interoperability means ability of two or more computer systems hardware or software to exchange information at the same type, each of the system is able to interpret the receiving accurate information by its original meaning. In this research, target of proposed model is to enable business values chain activities in sharing their data, information, and service to each other.

Level of Conceptual Interoperability Model (LCIM) is concerned to understand interoperability in detail. LCIM was first introduced by (Tolk & Muguira, 2003). There are five levels of interoperability, which are system specific data (Level 0), documented data (Level 1), aligned static data (Level 2), aligned dynamical data (Level 3), and finally is harmonized data (Level 4). According to Turnitsa (2005), the level of Interoperability is achieved when a common information exchange reference model is applied.

2.6 Summary

The objective of this chapter is to study existing design and implementation models to identify the gaps. Chapter explored the current statistics by research agencies reflecting the current trends in SOA adaptation. SMEs cannot apply the higher levels of **Capability Maturity Model (CMM)** to define precisely its business processes, as SMEs cannot have enough data and experience. Moreover, they are restricted to their budget for investment in technology, and therefore have a limited possibility to design stable business processes. It covers a thorough and detailed review of existing work on SOA based systems.

Through wide literature survey, the existing different testing tools and evaluation methods for evaluating service based applications are summarized along with their limitation. Although, the reliability of SOA systems cannot be completely estimated, we can estimate the reliability to a larger extent by analyzing the SOA characteristics and identifying the corresponding requirements. Chapters cover a thorough study in this work to identify the characteristics and define a corresponding requirement. Significant work done in the direction of estimation reliability of SOA is also summarized in table.

This chapter discussed the prerequisites in integrating three core value chain activities. Firstly, the general review of three participated system i.e. ERP, CRM, and SCM are illustrated; their similarities between the system that support integration and their interoperability among the participants are also discussed.

Questions

Q1. Implementing SOA based system in organizations requires a clear understanding of the system, its legacy and the technology offerings. Elaborate the current trends in SOA adaptation in perspective of companies, developers and higher management.

Q2. Point out the challenges in adopting service based on-demand systems in current context.

Q3. What do you understand by Integration and Interoperability among Business Values Chain Activities?

Key Terms

B2B   Business to Business

CRM   Customer Relationship Management

CM   Conceptual Model

CSS   Customer Services and Support

CMM Capability Maturity Model

ERP Enterprise Resource Planning

MRP Manufacturing Resource Planning

SCM Supply Chain Management

SME Small and Medium Enterprises

SOA Service Oriented Architecture

References

- Amelia M., Louis G., Peter J. (2007). "EAI and SOA: factors and methods influencing the integration of multiple ERP systems (in an SAP environment) to comply with the Sarbanes-Oxley Act". *Journal of Enterprise Information Management,* Vol. 20, No. 1, pp 28–36.

- Ali A., Ghosh S., Allam A., Abdollah T., Ganapathy S., Holley K. (2008). "SOMA: A Method for Developing Service-Oriented Solutions". *IBM Systems Journal.* Vol. 47, No. 3, pp 377–396.

- Bakry A.H., Bakry S.H. (2005). "Enterprise Resource Planning: A Review and a STOPE View". *International Journal of Network Management.* Vol. 15, No. 5, pp 363–370.

- Bieberstein N., Bose S., Fiammante M., Jones K., Shah R. (2005). *Service--Oriented Architecture (SOA) Compass: Business Value, Planning, and Enterprise.* IBM Press ISBN-10: 0131870025.

- Boris S., Marten V., Sinderen, Dick Q. (2006). "SOA-Driven Business-Software Alignment". *Proceedings of the IEEE International Conference on e-Business Engineering (ICEBE'06).* Vol. 23, No. 3, pp 86–94.

- Danilecki A., Holenko M., Kobusinska A., Szychowiak M., Zierho E. (2011). "Re-SerVe Service: An Approach to Increase Reliability in Service Oriented Systems". *In: Parallel Computing Technologies.* Vol. 12, No. 3, pp 244–256.

- Fatima B., Rachid C. (2013). "SOAda: Service Oriented Architecture with a Decision Aspect". *17th International Conference in Knowledge Based and Intelligent Information and Engineering Systems,* Procedia Computer Science, Elsevier B.V. Vol. 22, pp 340–348.

- Florian I., Thomas F., Klaus M., Wegener. (2008). "Runtime Adaptation in a Service-Oriented Component Model",

Proceedings of the 2008 International Workshop on Software Engineering for Adaptive and Self-Managing Systems, SEAMS'08. Vol. 11, No. 3, pp 97–104.

- Francis G. M. (2009). "Real-Time Event Processing for High Volume Applications Using Star Rules". In proceedings of the *Third ACM International Conference on Distributed Event-Based Systems*, DEBS, Nashville, USA, July 6–9, pp 203–213.

- Fumiko S., Shinichi H. (2008). "Pattern-based Policy Configuration for SOA Applications", *Proceedings of the 2008 IEEE International Conference on Services Computing* – Vol. 1, No. 1, pp 13–20.

- Gable, G. (1998). "Large Package Software: a Neglected technology?" *Journal of Global Information Management.* Vol. 6, No. 3, pp 3–14.

- Gokhale S.S. (2007). "Architecture-Based Software Reliability Analysis: Overview and Limitations". *IEEE Transaction on Dependable Secure Compute*r. Vol. 4, No.1, pp 32–40.

- Goseva, Popstojanova K, Trivedi KS. (2001). "Architecture-Based Approach to Reliability Assessment of Software Systems". *IEEE Transaction Perform Evaluation.* Vol. 45, No. 2,3, pp 179–204.

- Goseva, Popstojanova K, Trivedi K. (2003). "Architecture-Based Approaches to Software Reliability Prediction". *IEEE Transaction on Software Engineering.* Vol. 46, No.7, pp 1023–36.

- Goseva, Popstojanova, K., Mathur, A., Triverdi, K. (2001). "Comparison of Architecture-Based Software Reliability Models". In 12th *International Symposium on Software Reliability Engineering*, ISSRE 2001, IEEE, Vol. 33, No. 6, pp. 22–31.

- Grassi, V. (2005). "Architecture-Based Reliability Prediction for Service Oriented Computing". *Architecting Dependable Systems III*, Vol. 2, No. 1, pp.279–299.

- Granebring A., and Re'vay P. (2007). "Service-Oriented Architecture is a Driver for Daily Decision Support". *Emerald,* Vol. 36, No. 5/6, pp 622–635.

- http://lresende.blogspot.in/2007/11/apache-tuscany-and-sca-at-soaworld-007.html

- http://ieeexplore.ieee.org/stamp/stamp.jsp?tp=&arnumber=159342

- Jacqui C., Marijke C., (2010). Towards an Information Security Framework for Service-Oriented Architecture, IEEE, 978-1-4244-5495-2

- Joyce E.H., Maude M., Marta R. (2010). "TQoS: Transactional and QoS-Aware Selection Algorithm for Automatic Web Service Composition". *IEEE Transactions on Services Computing.* Vol. 3, No. 1, pp 201–229

- Jianqiang H., Feng E., Jun L., Xin T., Guiping L, (2008). "SOA-based Enterprise Service Bus". *Proceedings of the 2008 International Symposium on Electronic Commerce and Security – ISECS,* Vol. 22, No. 3, pp 536–539.

- Kerrigan S., Schelven R.V (2009). *Enterprise SOA Governance in a Product Organization.* SOA Magazine. Issue XXXIII.

- Kostas K., Grace A. Lewis, Dennis B., Smith M. (2007). "The Landscape of Service-Oriented Systems: a Research Perspective". Proceedings of the *29th International Conference on Software Engineering Workshops (SDSOA'07),* Vol 23, No. 4, pp 108–116.

- Liam O'Brien, Paul. Jon Gray. (2008). "Business Transformation to SOA: Aspects of the Migration and Performance and QoS Issues". Proceedings *of the 2nd International Workshop on Systems Development in SOA Environments.* Vol. 3, No. 2, pp 35–40.

- Linthicum. (2007). "How Much Will Your SOA Cost?" *SOAInstitute.org.*

- Lorenzoli, D., Mussino, S. Pezze M., Sichel A., Tosi D. (2006). "A SOA based Self-Adaptive Personal Mobility Manager". In proceedings of *IEEE International Conference on Services Computing. SCC '06.* 18–22 -September, pp 479–486.

- Marks, E.A. & Bell, M. (2006). "Service-oriented Architecture A Planning and Implementation Guide for Business and Technology". Wiley.

- Markus M.L., Axline S., Petrie D., Tanis C. (2000). "Learning from Adopters Experiences with ERP- Success and Problems". *Journal of Information Technology.* Vol. 15, No. 1, pp 245–265.

- Mike P. Papazoglou, Willem-Jan van den Heuvel Re. (2006). „Service oriented architectures: approaches, technologies and research issues". *The International Journal on Very Large Data Bases*, Vol. 16, No. 3, pp 389–415.

- Mukhi N., Konoru., Curbera F.(2004). "Cooperative Middleware Specialization For Service Oriented Architectures". In Proceedings of the *13th International Conference on World Wide Web*, May 17–20, pp 206–215.

- Musa JD, Iannino A, Okumoto K. (2004). "Software Reliability: Measurement, Prediction, Application". McGraw-Hill, New York.

- Navabpour S., Soltan G. L., Malayeri A. A., Chen J., Lu J., (2008). "An Intelligent Traveling Service Based on SOA". *IEEE Congress on Services 2008– Part-I*, pp 102–120.

- Sharma, R. and Yetton, P. (2003). *The Contingent Effects Of Management Support And Task Interdependence On Successful Information Systems Implementation*, MIS Quarterly, Vol. 27, No. 4, 533–555.

- Singh H., Cortellessa V., Cukic B., Gunel E., Bharadwaj V. (2011). "A Bayesian Approach to Reliability Prediction and Assessment of Component Based Systems". In: Proc. *12th International Symposium on Software Reliability Engineering (ISSRE'01)*, Vol. 23, No. 1, pp 12–21.

- Sriram A., Srinivas P., Jai G. (2005). "Perspectives on Service Oriented Architecture", Proceedings of the *2005 IEEE International Conference on Services Computing –, IEEE Computer Society*, Vol. 2, No. 2, pp 17.

- Tsai W., Zhang D., Chen Y., Huang H., Paul R., Liao, N. (2004). "A Software Reliability Model for Web Services". In: *8th IASTED International Conference on Software Engineering and Applications*, Cambridge, Vol. 12, No. 3, pp. 144–149.

- Tolk A., Muguira J. (2003). "The Levels of Conceptual Interoperability Model (LCIM)". *In proceeding of IEEE Fall Simulation Interoperability Workshop*, IEEE CS Press.

- Turnitsa C. (2005). "Extending the Levels of Conceptual Interoperability Model". *In proceeding of IEEE Summer Computer Simulation Conference*, IEEE CS Press.

- Tyagi K., Sharma A. (2012). "A Rule-Based Approach for Estimating the Reliability of Component Based Systems".

Advances in Engineering Software. Elsevier, Vol. 12, No. 2, pp 24–29.

- Van Latum, F. (1998). "Adopting GQM Based Measurement in an Industrial Environment". *IEEE Software* Vol. 15, No. 1, pp 78–86.

- Wang W.L., Pan D., Chen M.H. (2006). "Architecture-Based Software Reliability Modeling". *Journal of System Software.* Vol. 79, No. 1, pp132–146.

- Wang J., Zhong B., Yu H. (2010). "Research and Application of SOA Architecture in the Operation and Management System of Oil Production". In proceeding of *3rd IEEE International Conference on Computer Science and Information Technology (ICCSIT), 9–11 July, Vol. 1, pp 493 – 495.*

- *Xing S., Minjie Z., Yi M., Quan B. (2013). "A Robust Trust Model for Service-Oriented Systems", Journal of Computer and System Sciences,* Vol. 79, No. 2, pp 596–608.

- Zimerman, O., Krogdahl, P and C. Gee (2004). "Elements of Service Oriented Analysis and Design: An Interdisciplinary Modeling Approach for SOA Projects". *www.ibm.com/ developerworks/library/ws-soad l/index.html*

- Zimmermann O., Milinski M., Craes, M., Oellermann, F. (2004). "Second Generation Web Services-Oriented Architecture in Production in the Finance Industry", In conference on Object-*Oriented Programming, Systems, Languages, and Applications*, OOPSLA, 2004 Oct. 24–28, Vancouver, Canada, pp 283–289.

- Zimmermann O., Doubrovski V., Grundler J., Hogg K. (2005). "Service Oriented Architecture and Business Process Choreography in an Order Management Scenario". In conference on Object-*Oriented Programming, Systems, Languages, And Applications*, OOPSLA, October 16–20, California, USA. pp. 301–312.

- Zhang M.W., Zhang B., Liu Y.(2010). "Web Service Composition Based on Qos Rules". *Journal of Computer Science and Technology,* Vol. 25, No.6, pp 1143–1156.

CHAPTER 3

Research Methodologies

Structure

Objectives

After studying this chapter, one can be able to:

- Understand different research methodologies.
- Understand how to evaluate and analyze the data from different methodologies.
- Understand how to conduct a pilot test.

Chapter Outline

This chapter outlines the various research methodologies for evaluating SOA based systems. There are several types of research methodology depending on the area of work and type of experiment and analysis required such as *experimental research, observation research, specialized research, survey research, single-subject research*, and so on. According to Bordens and Abbott (2008), each of the type represents different way of collecting and analyzing empirical evidence by following its logic.

3.1 Introduction

Research methodology is the systematic way of solving the research problem. It is a science of studying how research is conducted scientifically. According to Holme et al. (1997), methods are a tool that can help to solve problems and reach new knowledge.

In order to meet the various objectives of the business, a number of sub objectives and correlated factors have been selected for the purpose. The factors relevant for designing such a model were gathered from a number of conference proceedings, past reviews research papers, records of selected organizations, and so on. Some of the factors surfaced after detailed discussions with IT practitioners and randomly selected respondents working at the three different levels of the management in the organizations. To test the validity of a model primary data can be collected using questionnaire-cum-interview method and then analyzed using statistical method.

Survey Research is the research methodology used in this book to understand the sample research study. It is used due to its suitability to the research objectives. In addition, survey undertaken was done in two modes during the course of the research i.e. survey questionnaires and interviews. In this chapter different methods of testing for validating the different perspective of the proposed model have been discussed.

3.2 Research methods

The study must be carried out with a view to identify the various gaps existing in the present business model for small and medium enterprises and to fill the identified gap with this present work. The proposed model would be helpful to rectify the shortcomings of the existing system. The study of the critical factors may help the organizations to use and implement the SOA system effectively within the organization.

Following methodologies can be used at different phases during designing and implementation of proposed model. *Survey Research* is at the core of each method used. Methodologies used are as follows:

- Interviews
- Survey Questionnaires
- Goal Question Metric Method
- Hypothesis
- Fuzzy Inference System
- Fuzzy TOPSIS
- Factor Rating
- Comparative Study

Our sample case study is exploratory as well as descriptive in nature. It identifies 14 factors that contribute towards the success and failure of proposed model. It provides an insight to develop an overall model for implication purpose.

3.2.1 Interviews

There are four types of interview structure: unstructured, structured, semi-structured, and group interviews. *If the goal is to gain an overall impression of a subject, then an informal, unstructured interview is often the best approach. However, if the goal is to get feedback about a specific issue/model then the structured interview is best method.* (Preece et al., 2002).

As the aim is to get both the overall understanding of the information system of enterprise and along with the perceived benefits and drawbacks related to them, hence, the most appropriate method is to conduct semi-structured interview. Researchers followed a Kvale (1996) method of conducting interviews that comprises of seven stages i.e. *thematizing, designing, interviewing, transcribing, analyzing, verifying and reporting.* In our case study, out of the seven steps, five steps are opted to validate the study (*Figure 3.1*), which includes:

Thematizing: Formulating a purpose of an investigation and describe the concept of topic to be investigated before the interview starts.

Designing: Plans the design of the study keeping in mind all the stages of investigation before the interview starts.

Interviewing: Conduct the interview based on an interview guide.

Analyzing: Choosing the appropriate method for analysis based on purpose and topic of investigation and the nature of interview material.

Verifying: *Ascertain* the generalizability, reliability and validity of interview findings

Figure 3.1 Semi Structured Interview

Kvale (1996) described that crucial point of interviews is the formulation of the question, so one could get the correct information to come to a conclusion. Otherwise one would have got biased in the answers, and would have been inaccurate for the study. Hence, all types of questions can be used in semi-structured interviews to get correct information in order to make appropriate conclusions.

3.2.2 Survey Questionnaire

In our research, survey questionnaire is chosen as the core methodology for data gathering and analysis. Because of the internet and technology today, not only collecting data through this method provides the most economical way of data collection in term of transportation but also result in reduced time. In general, survey questionnaire could potentially receive high respond rates from private networks due to ease of answering, editing, and analysis.

The respondents were selected irrespective of their gender from the top, middle, and lower level of management. The questionnaire covers dimensions of SOA implementation at Indian SMEs. To develop an effective SOA system, the various lifecycle phases like planning, implementation, stabilization, continuous-update, and performance are taken into account. The factors should be identified and included in the questionnaire on the basis of literature and discussions with the IT system analysts, system developer management, user management, and business analysts.

Three sets of questionnaires, i.e., Set I, Set II, and Set III were developed. The questionnaire prepared can be categorized into 3 sets as follows:

Set I – SOA design and implementation: Risk and Hindrance Factors

Set II – SOA system Implementation factors

Set III – Impact of SOA system implementation on business

The questionnaires are found in appendix. Number of factors are identified and considered for the relevant study.

Structured evaluation questionnaires are used to record the difference in the companies undertaken. Questionnaire design will be based on the literature study and exhaustive discussions with users and non-users of SOA systems. During pretesting of questionnaire the questions came as feedback and then these will be incorporated in final form of the questionnaire. Finally, the structured questionnaire would be floated in some of the companies. Self-structured close-ended questionnaire can be used to collect primary data. A five-point likert scale may be designed with each statement on usage of service-based systems having five alternatives to choose from designed in the manner given as follows:

- Value **5** represents **Very High**
- Value **4** represents **High**

- Value **3** represents **Moderate**
- Value **2** represents **Low**
- Value **1** represents **Very Low**

The likert scale is relatively easy to constructs compared to other scales. The process is to collect the large number of statements that meet two criteria:

i. To identify the relevance of the attribute being studied.

ii. To identify the favorable and unfavorable position of that -attribute.

Respondents would be asked to give the level of their agreement to the usage of SOA systems. In our case study, pilot testing was done on 30 respondents in totality at three levels in different companies. Later, final questionnaire was given to 245 respondents, but actual response came from 198 respondents which included 36 from Top management, 105 from Middle level, and 57 from Lower level.

3.2.3 Goal Question Metric Method

For designing questionnaire and metrics one can adopt a method from Van Latum (1998). The method works in three stages. At first stage organizational goals are identified in context of business strategies. In second stage, questions are raised that comply with the goal identified in first stage. The answers to these questions help to understand the critical factors and risks that may be associated in achieving business objectives. In third stage, metrics are designed to evaluate the model (*Figure 3.2– source Van Latum, 1998*).

In our study the last stage come up with the set of metrics which are capable to evaluate the proposed model. The designed metrics (questionnaire) was based on proposed model and then the responses were taken from industry persons. To evaluate it, average response was calculated. The industry people were asked to answer on 5 point scale, where each point has following significance:

- Value **1** represents **Weak** support
- Value **2** represents **Minimum** support
- Value **3** represents **Average** support
- Value **4** represents **Good** support

- Value **5** represents **Strong** support

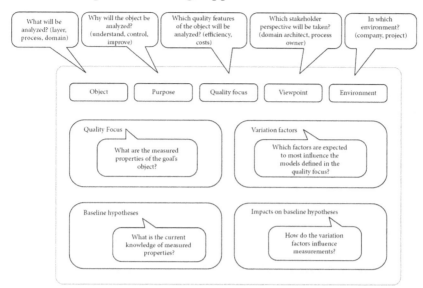

Figure 3.2　Sample GQM Abstraction Sheet

3.2.4　Hypothesis Method

Hypothesis method can be used to evaluate the acceptability of the proposed model. A hypothesis is a tentative statement about the relationship between two or more variables. A hypothesis is a specific, testable prediction about what you expect to happen in your study. Hypothesis predicts what the researchers expect to see, the goal of research is to determine whether this guess is right or wrong.

Let us define a following hypothesis in our case study to understand the application of this method and its significance in research.

Hypothesis:

"Proposed Integrated SOA Model is more efficient in terms of cost and adaptability than traditional ERP systems"

- *T– Test* is used to test the hypothesis that the two independent samples come from same normal population

3.2.5 Fuzzy Inference System (for reliability estimation)

Our case study also proposed a fuzzy model of SOA reliability based on the effects of ad hoc requirements, dynamic binding, agility, migration, legacy system integration, and business & IT integration. So far, most of the research on software reliability engineering focused on system testing and system-level reliability growth models. Approach for the reliability analysis of evolving software systems is well-illustrated in Musa work (2004). Significant work done in the direction of reliability estimation of SOA systems is summarized in *Chapter 2 (Table 2.5).*

Though the reliability of SOA systems cannot be completely estimated, it can be estimated to a larger extent by analyzing the SOA characteristics and identifying the corresponding requirements. Thorough study in this work has been done to identify the characteristics and defined corresponding requirements. Firstly, fuzzy inference system is used and defined it for the fuzzy logic toolbox for estimating the reliability of the system based on some factors. Next, an adaptive neuro-fuzzy inference system for more reliable estimation is used. The process and algorithm is discussed in detail in later chapters.

3.2.6 Fuzzy TOPSIS method (for optimal service composition)

Technique for Order Performance by Similarity to Ideal Solution (TOPSIS) is a well-known method for classical **Multi Criteria Decision Making (MCDM)** problems; many researchers have applied TOPSIS to solve **fuzzy multi criteria decision making (FMCDM)** and **fuzzy multi criteria group decision making (FMCGDM)** problems in the past with different approaches (Wang et al., 2007).

So far, the diverse techniques have been presented based on different points of view for performing service composition. Approach used in this research to perform selection of optimal service composition is taken from the algorithm proposed by Mehdi et al. (2012).

Services are core components of any SOA based application, we need service composition to answer different request. There may be a number of service compositions to get the requested task, and optimal composition of these services dynamically during runtime has always been an important factor of its success. SOA allow service brokers to execute business processes composed of loosely-coupled services offered by a multitude of service providers, and has been regarded as the main pragmatic solution for distributed environments. In such systems, each service may response the user request independently, however, many times we need service composition to answer different request and there may be a number of compositions possible to get the requested task done. Hence, it is important to find one composition which is best based on certain user preferences or criteria.

In our study, to identify one among the available alternatives composition, an optimal composition based on several criteria like functionality closeness, integration complexity, performance, execution time and task complexity have been selected. In this research, a novel idea for service composition in SOA is also proposed. The proposed approach is based on fuzzy multiple criteria decision making and used the **Technique for Order Performance by Similarity to Ideal Solution (TOPSIS)** based on the concept of positive and negative ideal solutions to find the optimal composition of services in any service-oriented architecture. The results obtained from experiment indicate the validity and efficiency of the proposed approach.

3.2.7 Factor Rating Method

In this method certain factors of adoption are identified on the basis of which decision has to be made that whether the proposed integrated model is efficient in comparison to traditional ERP or not. The factors are compared and analyzed on a scale of 3 in terms of difficulties that may face with the proposed model and traditional ERP systems.

- Value **1** represents **Low difficulty**
- Value **2** represents **Moderate difficulty**
- Value **3** represents **High difficulty**

The study of factor rating is discussed in later chapter which demonstrates the different factors of adoption with their score and weighted score. Based on the factors and their weighted score, their graphical analysis has also been done and is shown in later chapters.

3.3 Questionnaire

Survey questionnaire is mainly used to collect quantitative information about opinions or factual information based on the research objectives. It could be adapted by almost every research if not majorly then at least at the initial phase of data for analysis and identification of problem definition. (Campbell et al., 1953)

3.3.1 Designing Questionnaire

Designing a good questionnaire requires a systematic step to undergo while preparing and including questions for it. The steps followed to construct a questionnaire survey are as follows:

- Define a clearly objective of the study
- Identify a suitable title for a questionnaire
- Select the questionnaire format

3.3.1.1 Defining clear objective of study

According to Bordens and Abbott (2008), identifying a clearly defined objective will keep you to focus on the behavior or attitude chosen for study in the questionnaire. Further it is suggested to avoid too much focus in a single survey questionnaire that may leads to difficulty and sometimes ambiguity in summarizing and analyzing collected data in the future. In our research, after a thorough and careful observation of problem under study, questionnaires form are prepared and designed to conduct the survey. *Table 3.1* depicts the sample title and objectives of the survey questionnaire in this work.

Table 3.1 Title and Objectives of the Questionnaire

Title	SOA DESIGN and IMPLEMENTATION – RISK and HINDRANCE FACTORS
Obj. 1	To identify risk factors in SOA system implementation.
Obj. 2	To identify risk factors encountered with migration to SOA system.
Obj. 3	To identify risk factors in planning and requirement analysis.
Obj. 4	To identify risk factors in system design of SOA.

| Obj. 5 | To collect opinion regarding operation and security implementation of SOA system. |
| Obj. 6 | To get better understanding and opinion if other risk factors exists. |

Each objective comprises of set of questions which target to fulfill particular objective. It is important that before the respondents start to answer the questions, research objective is clearly explained to them. In this survey, the respondents are expected to provide their experience and views on risk and hindrance factors that are expected during designing and implementation of SOA system in organizations.

3.3.1.2 Identify a suitable title for a questionnaire

It has been suggested by many researchers that it is always good to keep the title of your questionnaire more relevant and as close to area under study for which questionnaire has been designed. It is strongly believed that questionnaire title gives the first impression of your work and respondent who is filing the questionnaire would be able to understand the purpose of study.

3.3.1.3 Selecting the questionnaire format

Three types of questionnaire items were used in the questionnaire survey. Questionnaire forms were divided into sections, where each section may cover different type of questions.

- **Open-ended item**: It allow respondents to answer the questions based on their own explanation without being restricted by a fixed set of possible responses.

- **Partially open-ended item**: It usually includes partially open-ended questions that used to overcome the limitation of the open-ended and closed-ended questions.

- **Restricted item (closed-ended item)**: These types limit the respondents' answers to a fixed set of possible responses. Questions include multiple choice questions, yes/no questions, scaled questions (rate from scale 1 to 5 for example), and so on.

3.3.2 Distribution of Question Type in the Questionnaire

Questions within the questionnaire were distributed in different sections based on the particular aspect of the objective defined. For example, section 'A' used to gather respondents' particulars such as job title, company, location, and so on. It also ensures that the questionnaire responses were captured from different, position levels, areas, nature of business and companies. Section 'B' may provide more basic questions that are easier to be answered. This is particularly aimed to make the survey participants comfortable with the questionnaire so that the remainder of the questions will not to be difficult to them. Likewise section 'C' may focus on the detailed levels of system. In general the final section of the questionnaire allows respondents to give their opinions in open ended format. They are encouraged and provide flexibility to elaborate their answers. This is very helpful in analyzing and understanding the other dimensions of problem under study. *Table 3.2* shows distribution of different format questions into sections.

Table 3.2 Sample Distribution of Question Type in the Questionnaire

Section	Type of Question			Total Questions
	Open Ended	Close Ended	Partially open Ended	
A	0	3	5	8
B	1	9	5	15
C	0	5	2	7

3.3.3 Conduct of Survey – Questionnaire Administration

Once initial study has completed and questionnaire is ready, the next step is to determine the target respondents for the data collection and most importantly to determine how to administer it. To achieve this, few methods can be used to distribute the questionnaire to the participant volunteers and get the responses from them. The method includes the following:

- Distributing the questionnaire in hardcopy
- Online survey
- Electronic mail surveys

Before the invention of internet technology first method was the only way to collect data from respondents. After the invention of **World Wide Web (WWW)**, now it becomes very easy to reach your target respondent. For survey questionnaire, online survey is assumed to be the best method. The significant advantages to using online survey include that the data can be collected easily and quickly, questionnaire can be created electronically and posted on the Internet through online survey service providers like *FreeOnlineSurveys.com, SurveyMonkey.com, GoogleDocs.com*, and so on.

In this research, Google based *docs.google.com* was used for survey. Through the given URLs, the participants from different companies working in different profiles can be invited to answer the questions by visiting the specified URL which are created for this purpose.

Another method to administer the questionnaire is through electronic mail survey. This method is little restrictive in nature as it involved selective respondents to participate. In this method questionnaire form will be emailed to the selected participants. One of the drawbacks of this method is that many of the email had move into junk mail automatically, and this reduce the response rate from the receivers. It is always good to attach a letter of introduction, definition and explanation of the survey with the email containing questionnaire. Finally, follow up mailings with additional words of encouragement to participate can also be sent out to the target respondents.

3.4　Data Collection

In our case study, data is collected from two sources:

  i. Secondary data collection (through literature survey)
  ii. Primary data collection (conducting interview and survey questionnaires from persons working in the SOA domain)

3.4.1　Secondary Data Collection

Secondary data can be collected through magazines, internet, journals, and research articles on the subject. The study can focus on reputed journals and websites of computer science, information technology, and information systems covering research articles on service-oriented computing, service-oriented architecture and issues related to SOA. This case study survey is limited to time frame from year 2000 to year 20011. This period is divided into three blocks to better analyze their growth and compare certain factors. The articles were searched with search term SOA implementation issues, SOA research, and so on. After filtering from total 200 papers, 95 articles and paper were identified that are relevant for this study.

It is identified through literature survey that SOA is evolving as organization are moving from their legacy systems to SOA environment, it is further identified that this growth is further expected to grow for the benefits that SOA provides and ad-hoc nature it provides to changing needs of business.

To analyze the collected data, it has been into theoretical studies and empirical studies. Theoretical studies are further split into illustrative, conceptual, and applied concepts. Conceptual studies describe structure, models or theories and provide explanation or reasons. Illustrative studies, basically try to guide the practice, offer recommendations for actions and explain action to be fulfilled whereas applied concept studies are a mixture of both conceptual and illustrative studies. They are mainly based on ideas, structures and speculations rather than on the systematic and direct observation of reality. Empirical studies have been divided into case studies and field studies.

3.4.2 Primary Data Collection

The primary data can be collected by administering the questionnaire to participating respondents. Five-point scale rating can be taken from the respondents by asking them to put a tick at one of the five-boxes. Respondents from the organizations who agreed to spend time should be invited for partially structured discussion. Some of the respondents should also be interviewed to gain understanding of SOA system in the organizations.

The case study adopted a descriptive type of research in which data can be collected from various sources and analyzed to come up with conclusion. Primary data can be collected by visiting industry person, communicating face to face, conducting telephonic interviews, mailing metrics designed through GQM and getting online responses through a questionnaire uploaded on internet using *googledocs.com.*

For this sample research, companies with 10 to 150 employees in the NCR region can be focused. The companies selected for the survey should be from various sectors such as manufacturing of automotive components, polymer items, electrical, and power equipment's, IT, industrial items, companies involved in turnkey projects. A sample of questions formulated for an interview can be found in appendix.

3.5 Pilot Test

It is the process to evaluate the validity of the questionnaire, or piloting the questionnaire. According to Bordens and Abbott (2008), this is an acid test as to whether or not the instrument that has been designed is comprehensive, clear, understandable, and complete with respect to what it purports to measure.

In our case study, thirty of the survey participants are invited to participate in pilot test for the designed questionnaire. The question in the test is designed to fulfill the following objectives:

- To determine whether the survey question is relevant, easy to read and understandable.
- Question do not contain any ambiguity and restricted type question have only one obvious answer.
- To guarantee that the question directly links to the problem in study and is meaningful.
- To test whether the question is too general in nature that causes the respondent difficult to answer.

Besides these objectives pilot test were done to assess the quality of the questionnaire, such as:

- Time taken to complete the questionnaire.
- Reactions of the respondent regarding instructions, definition of terms, content, and language.
- Whether response scale provide enough choices for responses.
- Any other opinions, comments, issues, suggestions or concerns.

3.5.1 Period of the Study

Case study primary data was collected from December 2010 to July 2014.

3.5.2 Sample Scheme

The respondents had been identified from various levels/business functions in each organization such as top management, IS management, functional heads, IT staff, and users. Respondents were asked to give the level of their agreement to the usage of SOA systems. The pilot testing was done on 30 respondents in totality at three levels in different companies. Later final questionnaire was given to 245 respondents but actual response came from 198 respondents which included 36 from top management, 105 from middle level, and 57 from lower level. The division of each level that took participation in our research is shown in the following graph:

Sample Distribution

Figure 3.3   Sample Distributions Among Different Levels

The primary data is collected through the questionnaire-cum interview method. It has been observed that increase in sample size will affect the results only marginally, whereas effort for it will be considerable. The sample size from a stratum had been determined on the basis of the following criteria:

100% of the population where sample size < 20

75% of the population where sample size >20

Tables 3.3 and *Figure* 3.3 shows the details of the sampling plan and its corresponding graph among different levels and different companies respectively.

Table 3.3   Sampling Distribution among Different Levels

S. No	Management Level	Popula-tion	Sam-ple	Actual Re-sponse	% of respon-dent size
1	Top Level	68	49	36	72 %
2	Middle Level	163	120	105	87.5 %

3	Lower Level	105	76	57	76 %

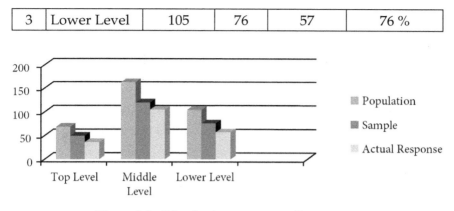

Figure 3.3   Distributions among Different Levels

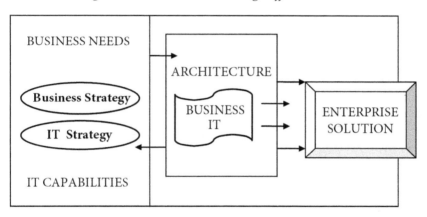

Figure 3.4   IT and business alignment

The study has been conducted to understand usage patterns and importance of alignment between IT and business processes in SMEs in India (*Figure 3.4*).

The SOA based model for integrating business values chain activities will concentrate on service discovery, service composition, and service granularity, defining **Service Level Agreements (SLAs)**. To analyze the study various SMEs were interviewed in NCR region and has been found that SMEs are bound with certain limitations, most important among which is low budget. Other limitation found by M. Sharma et.al (2010) are low capital base, inadequate exposure to international environment concentration of functions in one / two persons, inadequate contribution towards R & D.,and so on.

3.6 Summary

The chapter covers various research approaches used to evaluate SOA based systems. To understand the applicability of these methods, as sample case study is formulated for which primary data was collected by visiting industry person, communicating face to face, conducting telephonic interviews, mailing metrics designed through GQM and getting online responses through a questionnaire uploaded on internet using online survey platforms.

The content validity of the questionnaire must be ascertained before actually taken input from the different peoples. Various statistical and analytical techniques can be used in research at various phases to conclude results. The techniques include interviews, survey questionnaire, GQM method, hypothesis, fuzzy inference system, a fuzzy TOPSIS and factor rating method.

Questions

Q1. What is the significance of the *Pilot* test in any research?

Q2. What are the different sources of data collection? Find out the limitations and advantage of each method.

Q3. You are asked to propose a new design of an existing chair in your office. Prepare an initial questionnaire to collect user input to finalize your design.

References

- Campbell, Angus, Katona, Georgia. (1953). *Problems with Survey Research*. 1st edition, Transaction Publishers, New Jersey.

- Holme H., Solvang. (1997). *Differentiation Strategies for Operators sharing UMTS Networks*. Master's Degree Project, Stockholm, Sweden. pp. -100–101.

- Gokhale S. (2007). "Architecture Based Software Reliability Analysis: Overview and Limitations". *IEEE Trans Dependable Secure Computer*. Vol. 4, No. 1, pp 32–40.

- Goseva P., Trivedi K.S. (2001). "Architecture-based approach to reliability assessment of software systems". *IEEE Trans Perform Eval*. Vol. 45, No.2/3, pp 179–204.

- Kenneth S., Bordens, Bruce B., Abbott. (2008). *Research Design and Methods: A Process Approach.* 8th edition, Fort Wayne Press, Purdue University, Purdue.

- Kvale S., (1996). *Interviews: An Introduction to Qualitative Research Interviewing.* Sage Publications, California.

- Preece J., Roger Y., (2002). *Interaction Design: Beyond Human-Computer Interaction.* 1st edition, Wiley Higher Education. USA.

- Musa JD, Iannino A, Okumoto K. (2004). *Software Reliability: Measurement, Prediction, Application.* McGraw-Hill, New York.

- Sharma M., Mehra A., Jola H., Kumar A. (2010). "Scope of Cloud Computing for SMEs in India". *Journal of Computing.* Vol. 2, No. 5, pp 102–121.

- Van L. (1998). "Adopting GQM based measurement in an Industrial Environment". *IEEE Software.* Vol.15, No. 1, pp 78–86.

- Wang W.L., Pan D., Chen M.H. (2006). "Architecture Based Software Reliability Modeling". *Journal of System Software.* Vol. 79, No. 4, pp 132–146.

- Zimerman O., Krogdahl P., Gee C. (2004). "Elements of Service Oriented Analysis and Design: An Interdisciplinary Modeling Approach for SOA Projects". *www.ibm.com/developerworks/library/ws-soad l/index.html*

CHAPTER 4

Design and Implementation of a SOA Model – A Case Study

Structure

Objectives

After studying this chapter, one can be able to:

- Understand the basic framework of service-based model.
- Understand the life cycle of service delivery model.
- Understand the usage of Unified Modeling language in context of business models.

Chapter Outline

This chapter discusses the approach of SOA implementation and focus on identifying the factors of SOA system. It explains the layered approach in detail which is used to design any SOA based model. This chapter further highlights the advantage of an integrated model in comparison to traditional ERP. The chapter also highlights the system integration implementation environment, suggesting the software and hardware involved. It covers the unified modeling of the proposed model and present class diagrams for different business value chain activities.

4.1 Introduction

SOA is a style of design that guides an organization during all aspect of creating and using business services including conception, modeling, design, development, deployment, management, versioning, and retirement. SOA gives the ability to easily integrate IT systems, provide multi-channel access to systems and automate business processes. Moreover, SOA approach delivers a number of benefits including reduced time to market, improved business alignment for growth, reduced cost, and business risks. The core SOA lies on the concept of services, but SOA architecture is not only about services; it is a relationship of three kinds of participants: the service provider, the service discovery agency, and the service requestor (*Figure 4.1*)

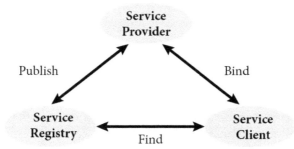

Figure 4.1 Basic SOA Architecture

The key functions, which the middleware must provide are **publish**, **bind**, and **find**.

Publish (Service Registry/Discovery). An automated discovery of services must be provided as it is undesirable to manually provide each component with a priori knowledge of what other services are available on the enterprise network.

Bind (Service Access Control). This coordinates authentication, authorization, and accounting functions.

Find (Information exchange). The user can find among various services published according to its need.

In today's competitive scenario where business demand changes very frequently, the expectation from technology has raised to a level where it is expected that the business processes can be developed in such a manner that they can adapt the frequent changes without affecting the overall organizational business architecture. Thus, the need of smart application arise that can be developed using service-oriented architecture in which services are loosely coupled.

4.2 Framework for the SOA based Model

Services are loosely coupled, autonomous, reusable, and have well-defined, platform-independent interfaces. Services can be written today without knowing how it will be used in the future and may stand on its own or be part of a larger set of functions that constitute a larger service. Thus, services within SOA are as follows:

- Provides a network discoverable and accessible interface.
- It keeps unit of work together that change together (high coupling).
- Builds separation between independent units (low coupling).

From a dynamic perspective, there are three fundamental concepts which are important to understand: the service must be visible to service providers and consumers; the clear interface for interaction between them is defined, and how the real world is affected from interaction between services (*Figure 4.2*). These services should be loosely coupled and have minimum interdependency otherwise they can cause disruptions when any of services fails or changes.

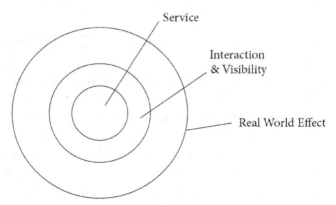

Figure 4.2 Service Model

4.2.1 Web Service Description Language Structure

Web Service Document Language (WSDL) document defines services as collections of network endpoints, or ports. *Figure 4.3* shows WSDL structure as presented by Thomas Erl. Hence, the following elements in the definition of network services are used in WSDL document:

- **Types**: A container for data type definitions using some type -system.

- **Port Type**: An abstract set of operations supported by one or more endpoints.

- **Binding**: A concrete protocol and data format specification for a particular port type.

- **Port**: A single endpoint defined as a combination of a binding and a network address.

- **Service**: A collection of related endpoints.

- **Message**: An abstract, typed definition of the data being communicated.

- **Operation**: An abstract description of an action supported by the service.

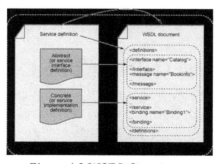

Figure 4.3 WSDL Structure

4.2.2 Service Design for Model

Service is an implementation of a well-defined business functionality that operates independent of the state of any other service defined within the system. It has well-defined set of interfaces and operates through a pre-defined contract between the client of the service and the service itself, which must be dynamic, flexible for adding, removing or modifying services, according to business requirements. From a dynamic perspective, there are three fundamental concepts which are important to understand:

- The service must be visible to service providers and consumers
- The clear interface for interaction between them is defined
- How the real world is affected from interaction between services (*Figure 4.4*)

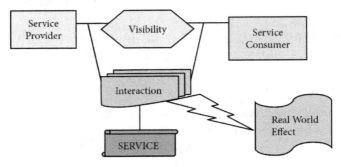

Figure 4.4   Service Model

In general, entities (people and organizations) offer capabilities and act as service providers. Those who make use of these available services are referred to as service consumers (sometimes service consumers and service providers are jointly referred to as service participants).

4.2.2.1 Service Delivery Life Cycle

Service delivery life cycle (SDLC) in context of SOA starts with service oriented analysis followed by service oriented design; service development; service testing and finally service deployment (*Figure 4.5*). Throughout this process Service administration is necessary to monitor the designed service and their orchestration for ad-hoc functionality. The task performed at each phase is as follows:

- Service-oriented analysis determines potential scope of SOA within the organization, Service are identified and mapped out from traditional legacy system to model as smart services.

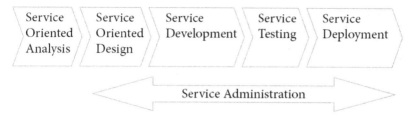

Figure 4.5   SOA Delivery Life Cycle

- In Service-oriented design phase, standards and protocols are designed conforming to **service level agreement (SLA)**, along with business processes.

- Service development phase is actual construction phase where services identified in design phases are coded using suitable -language.

- Service testing phase is required to undergo rigorous testing of services prior to deployment.

- Service deployment needs to configure distributed components, service interfaces, and any associated middleware products onto the production servers.

- Services administration is needed from service development phase onwards to keep monitor the designed services and their orchestration for ad-hoc functionality.

4.2.2.2 Service Design Guidelines

Key principles of SOA and services design are as follows:
- Discover services for business value chain initiatives
- Gather message information from WSDL
- Optimize SOAP messages
- Provide atomic services where transactions are needed

4.2.3 SOA Layered Architecture

According to Zimmermann et al. (2004) specifies quality attributes for SOA that cover reusable (well-crafted services), loosely coupled, cohesive abstractions, stateless, meaningful to business and standardized to comply with enterprise architecture patterns and underlying technologies. According to Ravichandran et al. (2007) IT architectural design features for SOA must include reusable components, modular, autonomous, i.e. capable of interaction and adaptability without human intervention, interoperable, and reconfigured flexibly in run time through service matching and dynamic binding.

Major modeling activities will concentrate on service discovery, service composition, and service granularity, defining service level agreement. These modeling activities can be embedded smoothly into an SOA reference model in the form of layers. Such reference model consists of minimal set of unifying concepts, axioms, and relationships within a particular problem domain and is independent of specific standards, technologies, implementations, or other concrete details (OASIS-2006).

SOA reference model and SOA layered architecture are used in present case study to design and implement our sample SOA based model. The explanations of the five layers SOA, used in model are as follows: (*Figure 4.6*)

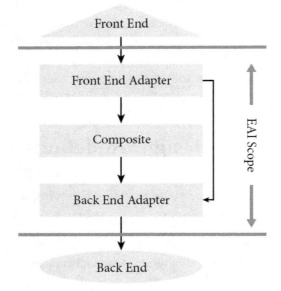

Figure 4.6 Five Layer SOA Architecture

- **Front End (FE)** layer represent the front-end systems of the ICT environment. Each front-end system can access one or more services through a front-end adapter.

- **Front End Adapter (FEA)** layer represent the services which offer their services to the front-end systems.

- **Composite** layer represents the services which combine the functionality of other services.

- **Back End Adapter** layer represent the services offered by the back-end systems. A FEA service always invokes another service, either on the composite layer or directly towards a Back-End Adapter service.

- **Back End layer** represent the back-end systems of the ICT environment. Each back-end system can be accessed by one or more services through a back end adapter.

An architectural strategy that helps achieve tighter business-IT alignment is well supported by service-oriented architecture by taking a three-dimensional perspective of the enterprise, viz. technology, people, and processes. The logical enterprise architecture of an SOA-enabled enterprise, proposed by SET Labs, Infosys' Research group is shown in *Figure 4.7.*

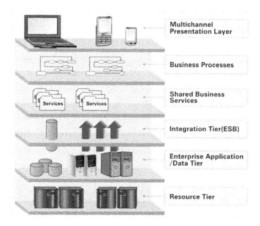

Figure 4.7 Logical Enterprise Architecture of an SOA Enabled Enterprise

4.2.4 Base Design for SOA Model

Figure 4.8 represents the base design of the SOA model used in current research; primarily it consists of service provider, service consumer, and service registry. A WSDL document describes the service details and need to be registered in central database, UDDI registry. Any registered user can search this registry for desired services and download the WSDL file. Through the information available in WSDL files the customer can contact service provider directly. All intermediary communication is done via a special protocol **Simple Object Access Protocol (SOAP)**, which basically exchanges messages via TCP/IP.

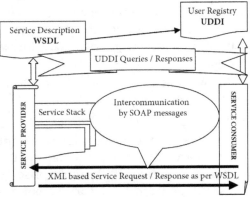

Figure 4.8   SOA Base Model

4.2.4.1 Service Integration in Proposed Model

In the proposed model, the services corresponding to business objectives are identified and are placed in the repository using WSDL protocol. These services are orchestrated dynamically to define business process. The architecture itself is ad-hoc in nature and if, at any time there is a change in business process, the services can be intelligently orchestrated dynamically to comply with new business process.

In our sample architecture, on the left accesses the service registry to discover another service and interaction is done by sending a message; consider an example of placing an order. This message is often part of a longer conversation between the services. For example, an order followed by an acknowledgement, an invoice, payment notice, and so on. For security, some of these messages might be encrypted, or require authentication.

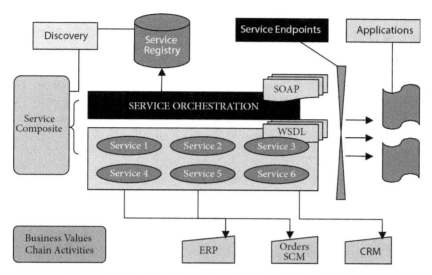

Figure 4.9 Service Integration of Value Chain Activities

In the *figure 4.9*, the service provider is a composite service (composite service refers to service that uses other services to fulfill its responsibilities). For example, an order service might need to access inventory or pricing services in order to accept an order or issue a quote. The task of implementing such a composite service is frequently performed by an orchestration engine, an element optimized to execute a multi-step process, which include interaction with other services. A rules engine may be appended in the architecture to guide the orchestration engine in the execution of the process by incorporating business rules. The endpoint manages the translation between the asynchronous world of messaging and the synchronous application program. As separate applications and services use data in different format which may be incompatible, a translation of the message is handled along the way.

4.2.4.2 Layered View of Proposed Model

At the front end, there is a presentation layer which takes care of the front-end user interaction. At the next, the business layer maps to composite layer in five layered architecture. This layer is sub layered to service layer and business model layer. The service layer comprises of all the services that are identified during analysis phase and are meaningful to the business. Business model layer defines the business processes and organizational business strategy.

In Nutshell, Business layer performs the service orchestration task as per the business strategy. In layered architecture, the communication flows only within the two adjacent layers and no layer over cross the other layer. Thus, business layer is accessed only through presentation layer and the business model layer in turn accessible only through the service layer. The back-end layer in the model reflects the data layer that directly interacts with the business layer at one end and database at the other (*Figure 4.10*).

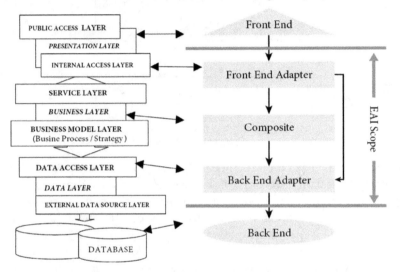

Figure 4.10   Mapping of Five Layers of SOA with the Layers of Proposed Model

4.2.4.3 Prospective Implementation of each Layers in Proposed Model

The prospective technology that can be used at each layer for its effective implementation is as follows (*Figure 4.11*).

- Presentation layer can be implemented by using any of the web technologies like Struts, JSP, ASP.Net, and so on.

- Business layer can be implemented using J2EE beans, servlets. Components can be designed using .Net Framework.

- Data layer can be implemented by using databases like Oracle, Sql Server, DB2, and so on.

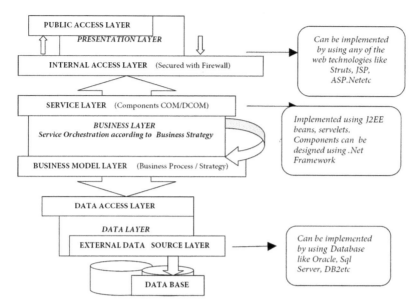

Figure 4.11 Mapping of each Layer with Corresponding Technology used for its Implementation

4.2.5 Enterprise Service Bus for the proposed model

The two significant options for a primary integration pattern are as follows:

  i. Direct point-to-point

  ii. Hub-and-spokes

In the direct point-to-point approach, each connection between applications (i.e., each service user-provider interaction) is individually designed and cooperatively implemented, deployed, and administered. In the hub-and-spoke approach, the interaction between service users and providers is mediated by brokering software. (Bianco et al., 2007), it provides a simplified comparison of ESB and point-to-point integration topologies. It is common in large organizations to have a mixture of approaches that depend on a variety of factors, such as application age and purpose of integration connectivity.

4.2.6 Architectural view of proposed Integrated Model

The architectural view of integrated SOA model is shown in *figure 4.12*. The figure shows the SME at the center of the figure and the specific process within the company is shown as business value chain activities. The primary process initiates with customer request for a particular service followed by order processing, material logistics, merchandise management and procurement and finally terminate with an eventual customer service.

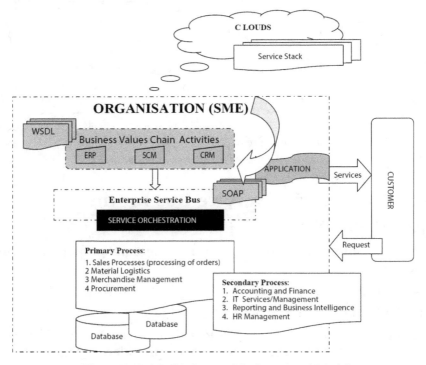

Figure 4.12   Architecture of the Integrated Model

The secondary processes shown within the figure are intermediate process that are necessary and are required to maintain the business. In order to provide customer with a service (application) needed, the company may use either their own inbuilt services or can share services available on clouds. The sequencing and interfacing within service to produce desired output is handled by enterprise service bus which is responsible for service orchestration.

4.2.7 Framework implementation

The description of the framework is shown in *figure 4.13*. The services corresponding to business objectives are identified and are placed in the repository using WSDL protocol. These services are orchestrated dynamically to define business process. The architecture itself is ad-hoc in nature and if at any time there is a change in business process, the service is intelligently orchestrated dynamically to comply with new business process.

Service repository contains the stack of services for business value chain activities corresponding to SCM, CRM, and ERP. Enterprise service bus accesses the service registry to discover and integrate the services, interaction is done by sending a message; consider an example of placing an order. This message is often part of a longer conversation between the services. The key benefits to implement integration using ESB are avoiding failure caused by single centralized broker, less development time and cost since more configuration than integration construction in ESB implementation, one time application integration configuration to provide ready for reuse service type, this enable same services used in different purposes.

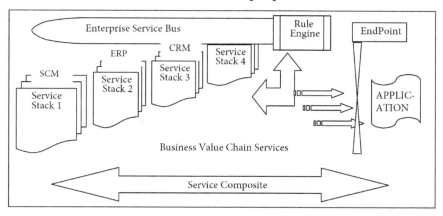

Figure 4.13   Framework Business Value Chain Services Integration

4.2.7.1 Service Orchestration

Let us assume that particular task is accomplished with the integration of several independent services executed in a particular order, this acquired task is defined in rule engine, Later at any point of time if customer requirement changes, and so the business demand, may result in change in the execution order of these services to accomplish same desired task, the only requirement is to train the rule engine in such a way that it can frame the rules dynamically, and can be capable to fulfill ad-hoc requirements. For example, consider that the task X is achieved by the execution of services x1, x2, x3, x4, and x5 in order and because of changed business requirement the same task will now be achieved by rather different execution order of same set of services, this can be achieved dynamically if rule engine is trained to adapt adhoc changes (*Figure 4.14*).

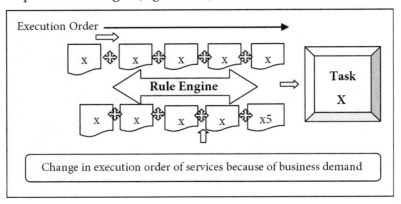

Figure 4.14 Service Orchestration and Execution Order

4.3 Unified Modeling of proposed integrated model

In this case study, UML and object-oriented analysis method were used to analyze business modeling value chain activities, the model can enhance the exchange among the experts, software designers, and users, making system develop smoothly. According to Chang et al. (2001), *It is very hard for ERP systems to perform real time simulation of adjustments due to constraints in the manufacturing, finance, distribution, warehouse or other operations because the system is mainly concerning on the business transaction processing*. Meanwhile, Robinson et al. (2001) stated that customer services must be directly connected to ERP systems in order to react rapidly to customer orders.

Considering these researches, it is very obvious that any isolated system be it ERP, SCM, CRM, though very efficient in its own is not good enough to improve the competitive advantages due to lack of collaboration among the company, customers and suppliers in the business context. These systems need to be integrated with each other in order to cater with continuous changes in business over a period.

It is really difficult to integrate the systems that are designed to work independently for attaining particular functionality done, for example SCM, CRM, and ERP, and so on. these systems are not designed to work together. More generally, the integration between ERP and CRM can be defined as a medium to collaborate front-end and back office operation of an organization that applied them. They enable customers and business partner to be included into value chain inward to and outward from the organization and encourage the collaboration between companies. It is also identified by Chen C.K. (2011) that in this era of competitive business world SCM, CRM, and ERP has become the most influential enterprise systems in term of improving competitive advantages of an organization. But it is also found that these systems running in companies are continuing to exist in isolation and become less relevant in today business context due to lack of integrated information achievable through each of the system respectively.

The main objective of this book is to present a design and implementation service-based model that enables interoperability among business value chain activities for any SME. Though many of the commercial integration tools exist today like SAP Exchange Infrastructure, Microsoft BizTalk and Server Oracle Enterprise Service Bus but they all provide less focuses on integration methodology based on service-oriented architecture. The research is focused on the development and implementation of the system that can integrate components in the selected systems.

4.3.1 Unified modeling language

The **Unified Modelling Language** (**UML**) is a family of graphical notations, backed by a single meta-model that help in describing the designing software systems, particularly software systems built using the **object oriented** (**OO**) style. Graphical modelling languages have been around in the software industry for a long time. The fundamental driver behind them is that programming languages are not a high enough level of abstractions to facilitate discussions about designs. UML is a relatively open standard, controlled by the **Object Management Group** (**OMG**), an open consortium of companies. (Rambaugh J. et al., 2005)

4.3.2 Use Case

Use case modeling makes the user understand how the system works through the relationships between actors and use cases. Use case modeling is user based and a function-oriented analysis method. It is quite effective as the requirements analysis method.

Use-Case analysis is a process of identifying the conceptual items and properties necessary for a solution to be both correct and proper. The use-case model describes what the system does for each type of user. The actors are entities that interact with the system, and the use cases are complete functionalities as perceived by an actor. As an example, the following *figure 4.15* shows a simple-first level use case diagram for simple buying and selling scenario where the buyer and sellers are the major actors of the system.

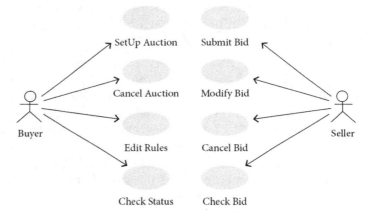

Figure 4.15 Use Case for Buying-Selling Scenario

4.3.2.1 Class diagrams for customer relationship management

In today's global trading environment, a flexible and robust customer data model is needed to capture customer's information to keep track of their behavior, to interact with them and prospect potential customers in order to forecast what their customer's trend will be in future.

There has been much work done in domain-specific areas, such as analysis patterns for Accounting (Fernandez et al., 2006), Reservations (Fowler, 1997), and Course Management for educational settings (Yuan, 2006). The following section describes some aspects of recording information about customers for an organization in a trading community that sells item to its customers, item may be any product or any kind of service. A trading community is defined as a group of entities taking part in some type of commerce. It includes persons and organizations. Besides seller and buyer, entities in a trading community can be Partner, Contractor, Distributor, Dealer, Agent, Influencer, and so on. (*Figure 4.16*)

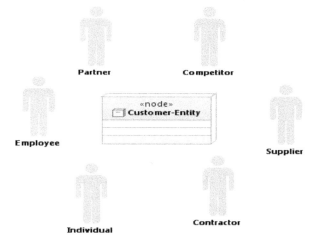

Figure 4.16 Customer entities in trading community

Companies or organizations need to interact with these entities to operate their business. Customer relationship has a broader context than classical customers, not only it represents the customer model; it also represents multiple organizations and multiple relationships that exist in a complex matrix-like environment (Fullerton, 2008).

A more generic customer model must reflect their prospective customer and their relationship with them; these relationships may be dynamic and can change at any time. Use case diagram representing the model are depicted in *figure 4.17*. Actor can be any individual or a company, relationship links to two entities to indicate the nature of relationship between them. Examples of such relationship are: supplier to /distributor for, client of/contractor to, report to/ manager of, customer of/seller to, and so on.

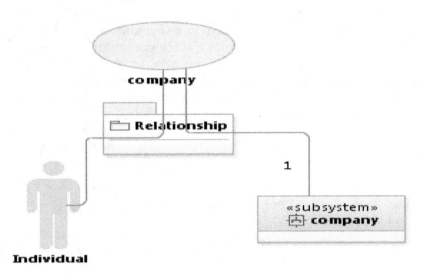

Figure 4.17 Use Case Diagram for Customer Relationship

Use case diagrams address the business processes that the system will implement. The Use Case is further used to identify classes to be represented in a UML and helps in establishing a relationship among classes in class diagram. The following class diagram shown in Figure 4.18 depicts the relationship between the two entities (buyer and seller). The company relationship may be either business to business (B2B) or business to customer (B2C).

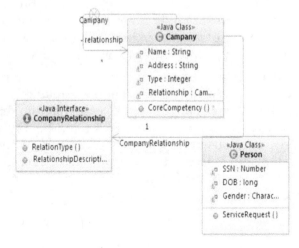

Figure 4.18 Class Diagram for Relationship among Business Entities

After coming up with set of use cases, an analysis level class diagram is shown *figure 4.19*. The classes are identified by examining the nouns in the statement. **Company** represents any business entities that can either an individual or an organization doing business. **Relationship** links to itself indicating the entities involved between a business deal. **Location** is essentially the physical location of all such business entities. **CompanyRelationShip** links two business entities to indicate the nature of relationship between them, regardless of their type. **Person** is an individual entity who is involved in any sort of business and takes care of personal details. **CustomerInfo** uniquely identifies links through **CompanyRelationship, communicationPoint** is an identifier for a point of contact to an any sort of customer. **CustomerPattern** take care of keeping and identifying the customer behavior and keeping information about changing customer trends over time, it is linked though **CustPattern** through **CompanyRelationShip.**

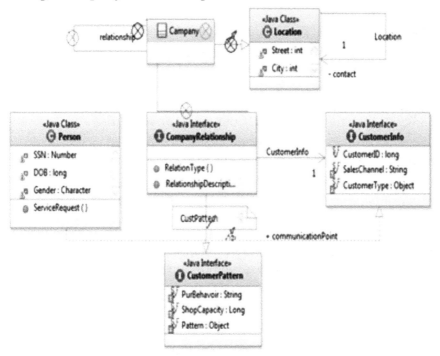

Figure 4.19 Class Diagram for Customer Relationship

4.3.2.2 Class Diagrams Supply Chain Management

Supply chain activities cover everything from product development, sourcing, production, and logistics, as well as the information systems needed to coordinate these activities. SCM spans a movement and storage of raw materials, work in progress inventory, and finished goods from point of origin to point of consumption (Agrawal, 2002).

To achieve a SCM system, retailer needs to manage the supply chain effectively and apply IT to system such as communications technology, computer technology. In order to promote the SCM, retailer must establish a management system. System model must be established before the establishment of management system (Haibo, 2008).

4.3.3 Analysis and modeling of business processes in retail system using UML

This work helps to automate the business process exist in any small and medium enterprises and covered the detailed supply chain transactions and customer management information, this will speed up the supply chain process and manage customer information to forecast what their customer's trend will be in future.

4.3.3.1 Use Case Analysis

Use case diagrams address the business processes that the system will implement. Use cases describe the functional capabilities of the system and the external actors that interact with it (Kopczak et al., 2003). Procure of goods is an important activity in any business system, normally this task is handled by retailer's purchasing department. The procurement process links members in the supply chain. Effective procurement contributes to the competitive advantage of a retailer. Typical procurement process includes the following stages:

- According to the user's need purchasing department set up purchasing plan and formulate expenditure which is delivered to financial department (Kopczak et al., 2003).

- Purchasing department transmit purchase documents to suppliers. **Electronic data interchange (EDI)**, which involves the electronic transfer of purchase documents between the buyer and seller, can help shorten order cycle time. EDI transactions, particularly through the Internet, will increase over the next several years (Angulo, et al., 2004).

- Warehouse department receipt/inspection/in storage goods and delivery warehouse warrant to financial department.

- Financial department formulate account receivable according invoice.

Based on the process of procurement management, use case can be identified and procurement management model be drawn as shown in *Figure 4.20*.

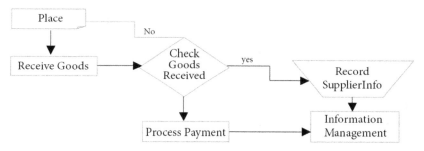

Figure 4.20 Procurement Process

4.3.3.2 Model for Procurement Management

This model represents the procurement process and emphasizes the flow of control among objects and models the function of a system. This models also simulates to activity diagram for procurement -management.

4.3.3.3 Class diagram for retailer system

The diagram shown in *figure 4.21*, describes the retailer system and showcase how different types of object and data element involved in the system along with the relationships that exist among them. This class diagram is a conceptual diagram and is free from any structural implementations.

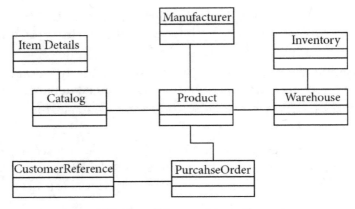

Figure 4.21 Class Diagram for retailer systems

4.3.3.4 Transaction Sequence of Goods Purchase

This is a dynamic model of a system; Systems dynamic behavior can be described using UML dynamic modeling. UML dynamic models can be represented by sequence diagram, collaboration diagram, activity diagram and state chart diagram, these dynamic diagrams describe object behavior and interactions between objects from different perspective. Following is the transaction sequence diagram for goods purchase: (*Figure 4.22*)

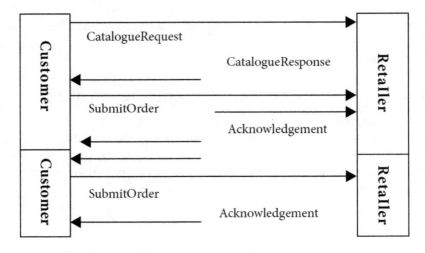

Figure 4.22 Transaction Sequence of Goods Purchase

4.3.3.5 Transaction sequence of source goods

This dynamic model describes the interaction between the retailer service and warehouse services. Retailer request to different warehouses for shipping goods, consequently the warehouse responds if it is in the capacity to fulfill the desired request. (*Figure 4.23*)

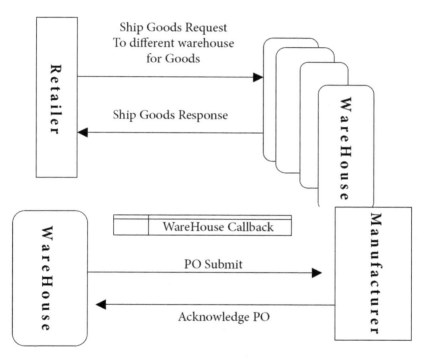

Figure 4.23   Transaction Sequence of Replenish Stocks

4.3.3.6 Transaction sequence of replenish stocks

This dynamic model shows the interaction between warehouse and the manufacturer. If any of the warehouses is unable to fulfill the desired shipping request, it further interacts with the respective manufactures by submitting purchase order (POSubmit), manufacturer acknowledges in response to it. (*Figure 4.24*)

4.4 Summary

The objective of this chapter is to design and simulate a service-based system that enables interoperability among business value chain activities of any SME. This chapter focuses on the development and implementation of the system that can integrate components in the selected systems (i.e. ERP, CRM, and SCM). In order to understand the overall integrated systems, chapter explored the concept of UML to represent the overall business values chain integrated architecture. The layered architecture of SOA is discussed and then the design of proposed model is explained in detail. Prospective technology used for implementation of model is explained. The unified modeling of proposed modeling is explained in detail with suitable examples.

Questions

1. Discuss the various components of layered architecture.

2. Using unified modeling language, propose a use cases for withdrawing money from ATM machine.

3. What are the benefits of layered architecture? Point out the limitations and challenges of such architecture.

References

*   Agrawal N., Smith S., Tsay A. (2002). "Multi-Vendor Sourcing in a Retail Supply Chain," *Production & Operations Management*. Vol. 11, No. 2, pp 157–182.

*   Angulo A., Nachtmann H., Waller M. (2004). "Supply Chain Information Sharing in a Vendor Managed Inventory Partnership" *Journal of Business Logistics*. Vol. 25, No.1, pp 101–121.

*   Bianco P., Kotermanski R., Merson P. (2007). *Evaluating a Service-Oriented Architecture*. Carnegie Mellon University. 2nd edition CMU/SEI.

*   Chang Y., Makatsoris H. (2001). "Supply Chain Modeling Using Simulation". *International Journal of Simulation: Systems, Science and Technology*, Vol.2, No.1, pp 24–30.

*   Fernandez E.B., Larrondo M.M., Petrie T., Sorgente, VanHils M. (2006), "A Methodology to Develop Secure Systems Using Patterns". *Integrating Security and Software Engineering: Advances and Future Vision*, IDEA Press, pp 107–126.

- Fowler M., and Scott K. (1997). *UML Distilled, Applying the Standard Object Modeling Language*. Reading M.A., 2nd edition, Addison-Wesley.

- Haibo Z. (2000). "A Unified Modeling Language for Describing Supply Chain Management in Retail Sector". China (http://dx.doi.org/10.1016/j.jss.2005.05.030)

- Rumbaugh J., Jacobson I., Booch G. (2005). *The Unified Modeling Language Reference Manual*, 2nd edition, Addison-Wesley, pp 89–100.

- Kopczak L., Johnson M. (2003), "The Supply-Chain Management Effect" *MIT Sloan Management Review*. Vol. 44, No. 3, pp 27–34.

- OASIS *Referenc e Model for Service Oriented Architecture* (2006), 1st edition.

- Ravichandran T., Leong Y., Teo H., Oh L., (2007). "Service-Oriented Architecture and Organizational Integration: An Empirical Study of IT-Enabled Sustained Competitive Advantage". Proceedings of *International Conference on Information Systems (ICIS)*, Vol. 12, No. 4, pp 108–122.

- Robinson B., Wilson F. (2001). "Planning for the Market? Enterprise Resource Planning Systems and the Contradictions of Capital". *The DATABASE for Advances in Information Systems*, Vol. 32, No. 4, pp. 21–33.

- Thomas E. (2004), *Service-Oriented Architecture: A Field Guide to Integrating XML and Web Services*, 1st edition, Prentice Hall.

- Yuan X. and Fernandez. E. B. (2003), "An Analysis Pattern for Course Management". *Proceedings. Of EuroPLoP'03*, Vol 9, No. 4, pp 899–907.

- Zimerman O., Krogdahl, P. and Gee C. (2004). "Elements of Service Oriented Analysis and Design: An Interdisciplinary Modeling Approach for SOA Projects". *www.ibm.com/developerworks/library/ws-soad l/index.html*

CHAPTER 5

Study of the inhibiting and success factors in SOA design and implementation

Structure

Objectives

After studying this chapter, one will be able to:

- Understand different approaches of SOA implementation
- Understand the governance aspect of SOA
- Identify the critical success factors of service-based model

Chapter Outline

This chapter focuses on study of the critical success factors in SOA design and implementation. It covers aspects of SOA that need to be better understood in terms of their relevance of SOA evolution.

5.1 Introduction

Service Oriented Architecture (SOA) is a way of reorganizing software applications and infrastructure into a set of interacting services. In this chapter, the concepts behind service-oriented computing, and how the basic service-oriented architecture helps deliver service-based application will be discussed. It covers two aspects of SOA that need to be better understood in terms of their relevance to each stage of SOA evolution i.e. *governance* and *service granularity*.

Most organizations (whether educational, commercial, or governmental) provide services to customers, clients, citizens, employees, or partners. Developing a service is different from developing objects because a service is defined by the messages it exchanges with other services, rather than a method signature. A service must be defined at a higher level of abstraction. Service needs to be developed within a larger context rather than an object or procedure because it is more likely to be reused. In fact, defining service for reuse is probably the most important part of service orientation.

The major difference between service oriented development and previous approaches is that service orientation lets you focus on the description of business problem. Separating the service description from its technology implementation means that the businesses can think about and plan IT investment around the realization of operational business considerations, as represented by the descriptions, more so than the capabilities of any individual product or software technology chosen to execute the description.

Following are the factors that form the basis of motivation to adopt SOA:

- The need to respond quickly to on demand change of business needs
- The need to motivate reuse of technical assets across a larger -enterprise

These requirements form the basis to motivate migration to SOA, and require steps to optimize development and support costs, and call for the creation of standardized assets, that once created, can be run anywhere. For example, consider a situation where business requests rapid and seemingly endless minor changes in business processes that inherently require significant application level code changes within timelines that are very difficult to achieve. Benefits of SOA only can be achieved fully if one is able to answer the following questions:

- How to get started?
- Where to get started?
- When to get started?
- What is the return on investment (ROI)?

Services must be developed, not simply for immediate benefits, but also for long term benefits. The existence of an individual service is not of much value unless it fits into larger collection of services that can be consumed by multiple applications, and out of which multiple new applications can be developed. In addition, the definition of reusable service is very difficult to get right the first time.

5.2 Approaches to SOA implementation

Broadly it is found that there are two approaches of SOA implementation i.e. theoretical approach and empirical approach. It is further observed that most of the approaches are empirical based.

These two approaches be further categorized into different level. (*Figure.5.1*)

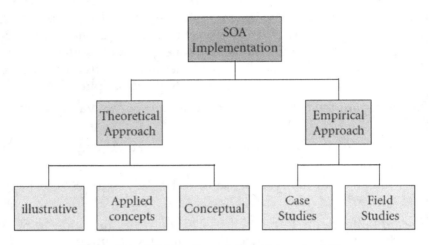

Figure 5.1   SOA Implementation Categorized View

5.2.1 Experiments and results to identify the implementation factors and approaches

In our case study, the information has collected from reputed journals and websites of computer science, information technology, and information systems covering research articles on service oriented computing, service oriented architecture and issues related to SOA. The survey is limited to time frame from year 2000 to year 2011. This time frame is further divided into three blocks to better analyze their growth and compare certain factors. The articles were searched with search term *SOA implementation issues/ SOA Research*, and so on. Out of total 200 papers, 95 articles and paper that are relevant were filtered out for this study. The *Figure 5.1* shows the number of articles published in different span of time.

The bar chart drawn for the number of research articles published during different interval clearly shows that the interest in SOA is increasing drastically. It was identified through literature survey that SOA is evolving as organization are moving from their legacy systems to SOA environment, it is further identified that this growth is further expected to grow for the benefits that SOA provides and its ad-hoc nature that handles the changing needs of business.

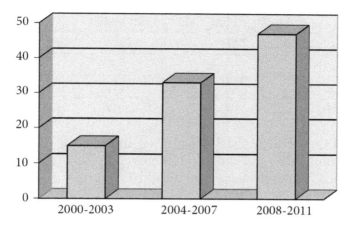

Figure 5.2   Number of articles/papers Identified on SOA Implementation

5.2.2 Identification of implementation approaches

To analyze the data collected for the purpose, it has been classified into theoretical studies and empirical studies. Theoretical studies were further split into illustrative, conceptual, and applied concepts. Conceptual studies describe structure, models or theories and provide explanation or reasons. Illustrative studies, basically try to guide the practice, offer recommendations for actions and explain action to be fulfilled whereas applied concept studies are a mixture of both conceptual and illustrative studies. They are mainly based on ideas, structures, and speculations rather than on the systematic and direct observation of reality. Empirical studies have been divided into case studies and field studies. *Table 5.1* shows the number of papers reviewed under different categories, out of total 95 papers, the majority of articles/papers found was empirical (52), compared to theoretical (43).

Table 5.1 Number of Paper Reviewed Under Different Categories

	2000-2003	2004-2007	2008-2011
Theoretical Approach **(43)**			
Illustrative	4	9	6
Applied Concept	3	6	4
Conceptual	3	4	4

	2000-2003	**2004-2007**	**2008-2011**
Empirical Approach **(52)**			
Case Studies	5	7	9
Field Studies	7	11	13
Total (95)	**22**	**37**	**36**

Figure 5.3 shows that most of the articles published are covering field studies followed by case studies. It is also analyzed that most of work categorized as theoretical got published during year 2004-2007.

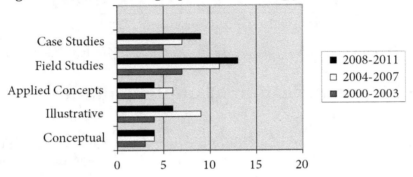

Figure 5.3 Different Studies on SOA Covered During 2000-2011

Similarly in Empirical category maximum work were found in year 2007-2011. It further indicate that among the theoretical studies, illustrative concept studies were most common followed by applied concept ones and the conceptual ones. The field study stands out as the most often used among the empirical methods.

5.2.3 Identification of Implementation Factors

Most of the articles/paper published on the area of SOA discussed the following factors (*Table 5.2*) that need to be taken care while implementing SOA. This research identified various factors in different papers and find out the percentage of each factor out of total articles published. The resulting factors were neither mutually exclusive nor collectively exhaustive; so an article could be classified into one or more categories and occurrence of given factor could increase with the increase in number of reviewed articles. The purpose here was not to rank various factors in terms of their importance but to identify and analyze critical factors of SOA implementation. Following table shows the number of articles dealing with each factor and the percentage of the total that they represent. Here total of each factor comes out to be 167, not 95, since articles reviewed may dealt with more than one factors. In *Table 5.2*, respective columns represent number of articles; their percentages out of total.

Table 5.2   Distribution of Factors year wise

Factors	*2000-2003*	*2004-2007*	*2008-2011*	*Total*
Governance Issues	6;3.5	10;5.9	8;4.7	24;14.3
Migration factors	5;2.9	8;4.7	9;5.3	22;13.1
Legacy Systems Integration	6;3.5	11;6.5	5;2.9	22;13.1
Change Management	3;1.7	4;2.3	4;2.3	11;6.5
Adhoc requirements	8;4.7	9;5.3	10;5.9	27;16.1
Resource Competences	1;0.5	2;1.1	3;1.7	6;3.5
Security Risk	2;1.1	3;1.7	3;1.7	8;4.7
Risk Management	1;0.5	3;1.7	2;1.1	6;3.5
Challenges in scope understanding	0;0.0	3;1.7	1;0.5	4;2.3
Integration Business and IT	3;1.7	3;1.7	5;2.9	11;6.5
Return on Investment	3;1.7	2;1.1	3;1.7	8;4.7
BPM and business agility	3;1.7	1;0.5	2;1.1	6;3.5
User involvement and Organizational Commitment	3;1.7	0;0.0	2;1.1	5;2.9
Training and Teaching Methodology	2;1.1	2;1.1	3;1.7	7;4.1
Total	**46;27.5**	**61;36.5**	**60;35.9**	**167;100**

Figure 5.4 show the pie chart of factors that are important for SOA adaptation. It clearly reflects the importance of SOA governance followed by issues of migration and legacy systems.

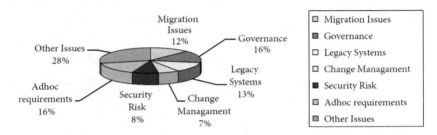

Figure 5.6　Proportion of factors that are mostly covered in the SOA article published during 2000-2011

5.3 SOA Aspects

The two aspects of SOA that need to be better understood in terms of their relevance to each stage of SOA evolution are *Governance* and *Service Granularity.*

5.3.1 Governance

Governance, in general, relates to consistent management and cohesive policies, processes, and decision rights for a given area of responsibility. It has different significance in respect to different domains. In respect to the area of IT, governance can be defined as *"the leadership and organizational structures and processes that ensure that the organization's IT sustains and extends the organization's strategies and objectives"* (Kerrigan et al., 2009, p. 2).

Software companies propose different perspectives on SOA governance (For example, SOA maturity models or service lifecycle management). Governance deals with policies and rules that the enterprise must adhere to while implementing SOA systems. The purpose of governance is to avoid lack of conformity between applications.

Understanding the business needs and capability of technology helps to drive the decisions within each enterprise towards creating a road map for implementation. Addressing the following set of issues may be helpful in achieving this goal:Identify the need to implement SOA

- Identify short-term goals and basic steps needed to achieve this goal
- Determine long term objective
- Try to elaborate return on investment
- Impact on business with a wider scope
- Complexities and problems in approach to change management

5.3.2 Service Granularity

Service Granularity refers to the scope of functionality that a service expose. Hence, it is important to go through the overall business process and understand the business environment. Only then can you plan and implement the granularity of the necessary services in a simple and generic way, based on your understanding of your current and foreseeable needs. To identify the level of granularity, one has to realize the overall business processes in terms of short term and long term objectives. The following set of questions can identify the short term objectives that can help to determine the granularity of services.

- Which of the business process are most frequently changed?
- What is the scope and how do you sketch a wider view to establish target architecture?
- What is the estimate of the work and timelines involved?
- What are the hidden issues of deployment of SOA?
- How best to determine the basic entities and functionalities?

5.4 Critical Success Factors

The software evolution has had distinct phases or layers of growth, these layers are built up one by one over the last ten decades, each layer come up with the improvement over the previous one and fulfilling the need of the time. As a general rule of thumb, CSF should target those things that affect quality, cost, customer satisfaction, market share, increased revenues, and so on.

Critical success factors have been used significantly to present or identify a few key factors that organizations should focus on to be successful. As a definition, CSFs refer to *the limited number of areas in which satisfactory results will ensure successful competitive performance for the individual, department, or organization* (Rockart et al., 1981). Success factors were already being used as a term in management when Rockart and Bullen reintroduced the concept to provide greater understanding of the concept and, at the same time, give greater clarity of how CSFs can be identified.

5.4.1 Aspects of CSFs

Rockart et al. (1985) have presented five key sources of CSFs: the industry, competitive strategy, and industry position, environmental factors, temporal factors, and managerial position (if considered from an individual's point of view). An industry's set of characteristics defines its own CSFs. Different industries will thus have different CSFs, an example of industry, and company CSFs was presented by Rockart et al. (1981) and is included here to illustrate their ideas (*Figure 5.5*).

The example presented is meant to illustrate that companies would have different CSFs and would not be completely similar. It can be seen though that many aspects of the CSFs could end up being similar for organizations in an industry.

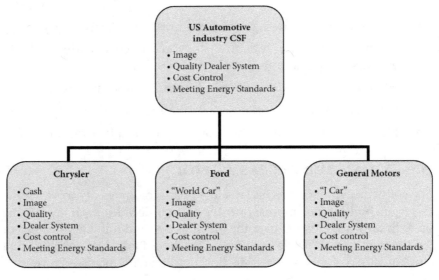

Figure 5.5   Industry and company CSFs

5.4.2 CSF in SOA Context

The studies merely focusing on SOA success do not provide adequate results that would explain how business-IT alignment is realized in SOA development. From a technological perspective, a successful SOA project may not fulfill the business objectives while still being successful in technical excellence. In such a situation, proper alignment is not achieved. Bridging the business-IT gap requires the following:

- A structured view of a business that facilitates its strategic and operational analysis and is a familiar representation to IT professionals

- A rigorous method to translate this structured business view to the appropriate (service-oriented) IT layer

- A new build and runtime technologies suited to the new IT layer (Cherbakov *et al.* 2005)

However, Luftman et al. (2007) argue, achieving appropriate alignment is not straightforward but involves consideration of interrelated components such as communication, value, governance, partnership, scope and architecture and skills. Henderson et al. (1993) argued that an organization's external fit is influenced by IT scope and system characteristics (reliability, flexibility and IT governance), and internal fit by the IS architecture, IS processes and skills required to manage and operate information systems.

Our case study identifies key factors to successful SOA implementation which include organization culture, SOA competency, team cooperation, governance, enterprise architecture, migration, change management, security, scope understanding, return on investment, and business agility (*Figure 5.6*).

Description of each of the success factors is as follows:

Organization Culture

- Organization culture has various impacts on the business alignment of SOA development. For example, when business and IT has to traditionally operate in a close cooperation.

- SOA development seemed to be better aligned with IT objectives (as expected) than in organizations where such cooperation was not a part of organizational culture.

Competences

- The skills needed in the design phase, such as business process modeling and service design, were considered particularly important for SOA application development. This was underlined, especially in the business process oriented projects.

Figure 5.5   SOA Critical Success Factors

- Service design was recognized by many organizations to be one of the most challenging parts in SOA development process.

Teams Co-operation

- Multidisciplinary teams, with members from both IT and business domains, were seen as crucial for SOA development.

Governance Issues

- SOA development was directed by defined policies and practices. This improved the quality of the SOA implementation by enabling a better fit with business needs.

- A generic SOA Governance model comprises a policy framework, organizational entities, a metrics system, and a catalog of best practices.

- Several software companies propose different perspectives on SOA Governance, including, for example, SOA maturity models or service lifecycle management. For IT Governance, many accepted approaches exist. In many aspects they provide guidance for SOA Governance frameworks.

Enterprise architecture framework

- The utilization of enterprise architecture framework was considered to improve business-IT alignment. With the framework, IT's capability to involve business people in systems development was increased.

Migration issues

- The problem that accompanies with major shift is that it threatens to make what already exists obsolete, even when existing systems represent massive investment.

Change Management

- The change management primarily deals with the strategies for the realization of new structures, systems, processes or behavior patterns.

- Key strategy to handle this is to first understand clearly the process of changes and then trace the changes.

Security

- Information security is to ensure that information security weaknesses and events are highlighted in a timely manner.

- Information security is achieved be implementing, amongst others, controls. For governance, control means to ensure that adequate measures are in place to provide assurance that objectives will be achieved and undesirable events will be prevented or detected and corrected (Veiga et al., 2008).

Challenges in scope understanding

- It is always very important to understand the architecture and the technology that is to be used in the right way and must understand and identify the capabilities it provides and what you can and can't do.

- Understanding SOA, requires a fresh approach, clear vision and a multi-dimensional view to understand the SOA scope. In order to undertake a project to develop a service or an application from services there is a need to know the scope and size of the work involved. This will help in determining the cost and effort for such a project.

Return on Investment

- Setting up the people, training, processes, tools, and components that fit into that architecture requires an initial investment and commitment from the development organization. Jeffrey *et al.* named this investment as the **relative cost of writing for reuse (RCWR)**.

- Based on data collected over the past 10 years, this investment is approximately 1.5 times (meaning 50% more) cost over building software for one-time use.

BPM and Business Agility

- **Business Process Management (BPM)** empowers a business analyst to align IT systems with strategic goals by creating well defined enterprise business processes, monitoring their performance, and optimizing for greater operational efficiencies.

- The BPM system provides a toolset that allows the business analyst to create process models, and then performs the business process automation, or execution of the model, by invoking the services.

5.5 Summary

Critical success factors are used by organizations to give focus on a number of factors that help to define its success. They help the organization and its personnel to understand the key areas in which to invest their resources and time. Ideally, these CSFs are observable in terms of the impact on the organization to allow it to have guidance and indications on its achievement of them. After reviewing large number of papers, it is concluded that CSFs can be utilized in both the organization and the individual levels.

In this chapter, thorough study of working SOA systems around different companies has been understood. Study reveals that some factors are crucial for SOA based systems. Factors were identified and percentage of criticality of each factor for the success of SOA systems are calculated based on the feedback and questionnaires submitted by different experts and researchers who are working in the same area. Key factors to successful SOA implementation include organization culture, SOA competency, team cooperation, governance, enterprise architecture, migration, change management, security, scope understanding, return on investment and business agility.

Questions

Q1. What do you mean by service granularity? How it is important in implementing any system.

Q2. Discuss various approaches of SOA implementation.

Q3. Identify two critical success factors for implementing SOA based system in small and medium enterprises.

Key Terms

B2B Business to business

BPM Business Process Management

CM Conceptual Model

CSF Critical Service Factors / Critical Success Factor

CSS Customer Services and Support

ROI Return of Investment

SCM Supply Chain Management

SDLC Software Development Life Cycle

SMESmall and Medium Enterprises

SOAService Oriented Architecture

UC Use Case

UML Unified Modeling Language

References

- Barrett H., Balloun J., Weinstein A., (2005). "Success Factors for Organizational Performance: Comparing Business Services, Health Care, and Education". *SAM Advanced Management Journal*. Vol. 70, No.4, pp 122–141.

- Chan Y.E., Reich B.H. (2007). "IT Alignment: What Have We Learned?". *Journal of Information Technology*. Vol. 22, No. 7, pp. 297–331.

- Cherbakov L., Galambos G., Harishankar R., Kalyana S. and Rackham G. (2005), "Impact of service orientation at the business level", *IBM Systems Journal*, Vol. 44, No. 4, pp.653–668.

- Henderson J. C., Venkatraman N. (1993), "Strategic Alignment: Leveraging Information Technology for Transforming Organizations", *IBM Systems Journal*, Vol. 32, No. 1, pp. 4–16.

- http://www.coursewrk4you.co.uk/essaysanddissertatio/criticalsuccessfactors.php

- Jeffery P. (1997). *Measuring Software Reuse* 3rd edition, Addison Wesley.

- Kerrigan M., Van M., Schelven (2009). *Preventing SOA Failures: Effective SOA Governance*, SOA magazine, issue XXIII.

- Lawler J.P.,.Howel H., Barber (2008) *Service-Oriented Architecture (SOA): Strategy, Methodology, and Technology*, Pace Seidenberg School of Computer Science and Information Systems.

- Luftman J., Kempaiah R. (2007), "An Update on Business-IT Alignment: A line has been drawn", *MIS Quarterly Executive*, Vol. 3, No. 6, pp 105–117.

- Rockart, J., Van Bullen, C. (1981). "A Primer on Critical Success Factors". The Rise of Management Computing. Homewood. Irwin. Issue 28.

- Seth A., Aggarwal H. and Singla A. R. (2012), *"Service Oriented Architecture Adoption Trends: A Critical Survey"*, *Contemporary Computing Communications in Computer and Information Science*, Vol. 306, pp 164–175.

- Veiga, A., Eloff, J.H.P. (2008). "A Framework and Assessment Instrument for Information Security Culture". *Computer & Security*, Vol. 29, No. 2, pp 196–207.

CHAPTER 6

Testing of Service Based Model

Structure

Objectives

After studying this chapter, one will be able to:

- Understand the different strategies to test and evaluate service-based systems.
- Understand fuzzy rule-based reliability algorithms.
- Understand fuzzy TOPSIS method.
- Understand various statistical techniques for analyzing and interpreting data.

Chapter Outline

This chapter covers an extensive discussion of the various methods used for evaluating different aspect of the service based system. It discusses the results of the following experiments:

Identification of implementation approaches.

- Reliability estimation of system using fuzzy approach.
- Reliability estimation of system using adaptive neuro-fuzzy approach.

- Evaluation of optimal service composition within a system using fuzzy TOPSIS.

- Evaluation of performance of proposed system using *factor rating method*.

- Evaluation of proposed hypothesis using T-test.

The detailed analysis of experiments and result is presented in table forms as well as in graphical diagrams. The results captured from the survey questionnaire are analyzed and summary of the findings are also covered.

6.1 Introduction

Several testing methods were used to validate the different perspective of the proposed model. To identify the important factors of SOA implementation, thorough survey of existing work that needs to be done. Survey can be based on information from industry sources, journal, web articles, and magazines. The experiments discussed in this chapter are from the top down and bottom-up analysis to ensure that sample model that we took for our case study will be good enough in all perspective. Fuzzy and adaptive neuro-fuzzy inference approach is used to estimate the reliability of the system and proposed fuzzy algorithms for reliability. Thorough study has been done to identify the characteristics of service oriented systems and define corresponding requirements. It started with the identification of important factors for SOA, followed by, estimating the reliability of such systems using Matlab fuzzy tool box. The algorithm for reliability estimation is discussed in detailed in the later section of this chapter. Moreover, performance of ANFIS with a plain FIS for similar data sets is also compared.

This chapter proposed a way for selecting the optimal services composition among several available feasible compositions, based on certain user criteria using Fuzzy TOPSIS. An approach is basically a fuzzy multiple criteria decision making, which is based on the concept of positive and negative ideal solutions to find the optimal composition of services in any service oriented architecture. The chapter discusses a numerical example and its evaluation using the proposed approach. Results obtained, indicate the validity and efficiency of the approach.

In our sample evaluation, a hypothesis has been proposed to evaluate the acceptability of the proposed model. Further, experiments were done to find whether proposed integrated model is efficient in comparison to traditional ERP or not. For this, certain factors of adoption were identified on the basis of which decision has to be made. The factors were compared and analyzed on a scale of 3 in terms of difficulties that may face with the proposed model and traditional ERP systems.

6.2 Experimental Evaluation for Reliability of System

So far, most of the research on software reliability engineering focused on system testing and system-level reliability growth models. Approach for the reliability analysis of evolving software systems is well-illustrated in Musa work (2004). However, SOA is not taken into account in any of these approaches.

After identifying the factors that are relevant to SOA implementation and the extent to which each factor is crucial to SOA implementation. First phase of work started with a set of questionnaires to identify the factors responsible for system reliability in SOA context. Using GQM technique, metric is proposed, and the responses were taken from 198 people in the industry. Based on the feedback and responses, factors were categorized into following three parameters:

1. **AR:** Adhoc requirements/dynamic binding/agility
2. **MG:** Migration/legacy system integration
3. **BI:** Business and IT collaboration

The rules were defined for the inference engine. Three clusters were formed for the input factors (Low, Medium, and High), and five clusters were formed for the output reliability (Very Low, Low, Medium, High, and Very High). Therefore, 3 clusters and 3 input parameters yield 33 = 27 sets. These 27 sets or classifications can be used to form 27 rules using fuzzy model.

6.2.1 Reliability parameters for SOA-Based systems with its constituent factors

1. **AR:** A system capable of fulfilling the adhoc on-demand changing requirement of the market is assumed to be efficient

and reliable. It is based on how the rule engine within the model has been trained to perform dynamic binding, when the demand change or arise. This also covers agility, which is an important issue when someone moves from present legacy systems to SOA-based systems. It is further concluded that systems having capability to handle dynamic binding/ad hoc requirement/agility are reliable, i.e.

SOA Reliability α AR.

2. **MG:** It has been observed that, though, a SOA system is strong enough in its own to handle ad-hoc market, if there is no provision to integrate the legacy system or migrate successfully from an old system to new one within the system; it is not effective. It will not guarantee reliability and systems are to develop from scratch. Thus, the system having capability to handle migration or provide legacy integration are reliable, .i.e.

SOA Reliability α MG

3. **BI:** It has been observed that, although the powerful IT system is there, it will not be of much value to the organization without proper integration within the business strategies. Within a system, if the collaboration between business process and strategies is aligned with IT capabilities, the system is assumed to be more reliable, i.e.

SOA Reliability α BI

The factors described in three parameters assess different properties and characteristics associated with SOA model reliability. The values of these parameters cannot be used independently to measure reliability. Rather, an integrated approach that considers all three parameters and their relative impact is required to estimate a system's overall reliability.

6.2.2 Fuzzy Rule-Based reliability algorithm

A fuzzy model of SOA reliability has been proposed which is based on the effects of ad hoc requirements, dynamic binding, agility, migration, legacy system integration, and business and IT integration. In this research work, initially, Mamdani-type inference system was followed, defined it for the fuzzy logic toolbox, which expects the output membership functions to be fuzzy sets. After the aggregation process, there is a fuzzy set for each output variable that needs to be defuzzified. The detailed algorithm is as follows:

1. Identify the factors that are crucial to SOA implementation.
2. Identify reliability parameters in SOA context among these -factors.
3. Cluster factors into three domain clusters of reliability -parameters.
4. Assemble a database for the value of these factors.
5. Design an inference engine based on the rule for identifying -reliability clusters.
6. Use Fuzzy logic, perform the following operations:
   a. Fuzzify the input variables
   b. Determination of membership functions for the parameters
   c. Application of the fuzzy operator (AND) in the antecedent
   d. Implication from the antecedent to the consequent
   e. Aggregation of the consequents across the rules
   f. Defuzzification

For defuzzification, centroid technique has been used to produce a crisp value in the range $[0, 1]$. For the SOA reliability index, a singleton output membership function is used. It enhances the efficiency of the defuzzification process, because it greatly simplifies the computation required by the more general mamdani method, which finds the centroid of a two-dimensional function.

6.2.2.1 Designing a Rule Base for the Fuzzy Inference Engine

Rules were designed by considering all the possible combinations of different inputs and reliability parameters (see appendix for the complete set of rule base). All 27 rules were entered to create a rule base. Reliability for all 27 combinations was classified based on expert opinion as Very High, High, Medium, Low, or Very Low. These classifications were used to form 27 rules for the fuzzy model. Rules were fired depending on the particular set of inputs, using Mamdani-style inferences.

6.2.2.2 Membership Functions for Input Parameters and Output Parameters

Membership functions (MFs) were defined for fuzzifying the application. An MF is a curve that defines how each point in the input space is mapped to a membership value (or degree of membership) between 0 and 1. Out of 11 built in a membership function type, we have used triangular memberships function; it has the function name *trimf*. It is nothing more than a collection of three points forming a triangle. The degree to which an object belongs to a fuzzy set is denoted by a membership value between 0 and 1. As an example, the input parameter AG was divided into three levels low, medium, and high. Degree of membership function for all input parameters and complete inference engine is found in appendices.

6.2.2.3 Output Computation of the Model

Let us suppose that we have the following input models:

Input1 = 7.5

Input2 = 6.2

Input3 = 1.8

When these inputs are fuzzified, we find that *Input1 = 7.5* belongs to the Low fuzzy set with membership grade .75; *Input2 = 6.2* belongs the medium fuzzy set with membership grade 0.25 and the High fuzzy set with membership grade 0.5, and *Input3 = 1.8* belongs to the Low fuzzy set with membership grade .5. With these inputs, rule 15 and 25 are fired. During composition of these rules we get the following:

Min (0.75, 0.25, 0.5) *= 0.25*

Min (0.75, 0.5, 0.5) *= 0.5*

When these two rules are implicated, we find that the first rule gives the low output to an extent of 0.25, and second rule gives the medium output with an extent of 0.5.

6.2.2.4 Defuzzification

After the aggregation process, there is a fuzzy set for each output variable that needs defuzzification. Centroid method is used for defuzzification, which returns the center of area under the curve. After obtaining the fuzzified outputs as shown in *Table 6.1*. They are defuzzified to obtain a crisp value for the output variable 'SOAReliability'. The **center of gravity (COG)** of the fuzzy output is calculated as follows:

$$\text{Output} = \frac{\int_0^{2.5}.25x\,dx + \int_{2.5}^3 (mx+c)x\,dx + \int_3^5.5x\,dx + \int_5^7 (mx+c)x\,dx}{\int_0^{2.5}.25\,dx + \int_{2.5}^3 (mx+c)\,dx + \int_3^5.5\,dx + \int_5^7 (mx+c)\,dx} = 4.3 \quad (1)$$

The effects of these rules were simulated with the MATLAB fuzzy logic toolbox; the reliability for the values above turns out to be 4.3, which is very close to the calculated value.

Table 6.1 Rule-Based Output

Input1	Input2	Input3	Output	Degree of membership for output
High	Medium	Low	Medium	Min (0.75, 0.25, 0.5) = 0.25
High	Low	Low	Low	Min (0.75, 0.5, 0.5) = 0.5

6.2.3 Adaptive Neuro Fuzzy Inference System Approach

The entire process is shown in following steps:

1. Identify the factors that are relevant to SOA implementation.

2. Identify reliability parameters in SOA context among these -factors.

3. Cluster reliability parameters into three domain clusters of reliability factors.

4. Assemble a database for the value of these factors.

5. Design an inference engine based on the rule for identifying reliability clusters.

6. Using Sugeno system, perform the following operations:

   i. Plot the number of inputs, outputs, input membership functions, and output membership functions.

   ii. Load FIS or generate FIS from loaded data using your chosen number of MFs and rules or fuzzy.

   iii. Train FIS after setting optimization method, error tolerance, and number of epochs.

iv. Test data against the FIS model.

v. Anticipate the FIS model output versus the training, checking, or testing data output.

Training data set contains desired input/output data pairs of the target system to be modeled. These training and checking data sets are collected based on observations of the target system and are then stored in separate files. Fuzzy *neuro-adaptive* learning techniques incorporated in the **anfis** command has been used. The parameters could be chosen so as to tailor the membership functions to the input/output data in order to account for these types of variations in the data values. Experiments simulated the effect of rules with the MATLAB fuzzy logic toolbox.

To analyze the result obtained from the experiment, covariance method is used to compare the closeness of the value obtained with the values collected from original sample data set. Covariance provides a measure of the strength of the correlation between two or more sets of random variants. The covariance for two random variants X and Y, each with sample size N, is defined by the expectation value.

$$\text{cov}(X, Y) = \langle (X - \mu_X)(Y - \mu_Y) \rangle$$
$$= \langle X\,Y \rangle - \mu_X\,\mu_y \tag{2}$$

where $\mu_x = \langle X \rangle$ and $\mu_y = \langle Y \rangle$ are the respective means, which can be written out explicitly as:

$$\text{cov}(X, Y) = \sum_{i=1}^{N} \frac{(x_i - \bar{x})(y_i - \bar{y})}{N}. \tag{3}$$

The comparison table for the ANFIS and original data set is shown in the *Table 6.2*.

Table 6.2 Comparison of Original Data Set with ANFIS using Sugeno Method

Input1	Input2	Input3	Original	ANFIS
0.0101	0.0101	0.0101	0.4321	0.4514
0.0202	0.0202	0.0202	0.4321	0.4503
0.0303	0.0303	0.0303	0.4231	0.4494
0.0404	0.0404	0.0404	0.4212	0.4486
0.0505	0.0505	0.0505	0.4321	0.448
0.0606	0.0606	0.0606	0.4251	0.4474

Input1	Input2	Input3	Original	ANFIS
0.0707	0.0707	0.0707	0.4421	0.4469
0.0808	0.0808	0.0808	0.4899	0.4465
0.0909	0.0909	0.0909	0.4548	0.4461
0.0101	0.0101	0.0101	0.4748	0.4458
0.1414	0.1414	0.1414	0.4321	0.4447
0.1818	0.1818	0.1818	0.4243,	0.444
0.2121	0.2121	0.2121	0.4889	0.4436
0.2525	0.2525	0.2525	0.6321	0.4427
0.2828	0.2828	0.2828	0.4521	0.4501
0.3434	0.3434	0.3434	0.4646	0.4706
0.3636	0.3636	0.3636	0.4436	0.4799
0.4747	0.4747	0.4747	0.5831	0.5932
0.4949	0.4949	0.4949	0.6321	0.6444
0.5455	0.5455	0.5455	0.5591	0.5692
0.5960	0.5960	0.5960	0.4999	0.5218
0.5758	0.5758	0.5758	0.5215	0.5371
0.6768	0.6768	0.6768	0.4652	0.4842
0.6869	0.6869	0.6869	0.4461	0.4811
0.7172	0.7172	0.7172	0.4142	0.473
0.7374	0.7374	0.7374	.04651	0.4684
0.8081	0.8081	0.8081	0.21	0.2314
0.8283	0.8283	0.8283	0.2121	0.2222
0.8788	0.8788	0.8788	0.1712	0.1913
0.8990	0.8990	0.8990	0.1744	0.1744
0.9292	0.9292	0.9292	0.1542	0.1533

Covariance matrix for (anfis, original) = 0.0137   0.0135

0.0135   0.0137

Average Testing Error is = .021%

Since the covariance is positive, it is concluded that the results obtained are closer to the original values.

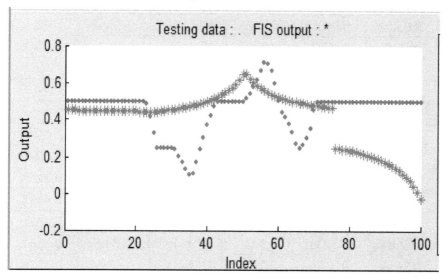

Figure 6.1   Plot of Testing Data: Original vs ANFIS

After creating the ANFIS model, the output reliability values for different input sets with the original values were compared. Average testing error for the output obtained by the FIS and the output obtained by the ANFIS with the original output is calculated. ANFIS reduces the error to .021%. Hence, the ANFIS performs better than the FIS. First trained the FIS using the ANFIS, the rules were formed on the basis of training data to produce the output of the trained model. The only limitation of this model is that its execution is complex for large data sets. Obtained results show that the ANFIS model gives more accurate measure of reliability than the FIS model. *Table 6.3* illustrates the comparison chart for FIS, ANFIS, and original. Graph shown in *Figure 6.1* indicates ANFIS is closer to original values than FIS.

Table 6.3   Plot of FIS, ANFIS and Original

Input1	Input2	Input3	Ori	ANFIS	FIS
0.0101	0.0101	0.0101	0.4321	0.4514	0.4
0.0202	0.0202	0.0202	0.4321	0.4503	0.4
0.0303	0.0303	0.0303	0.4231	0.4494	0.4
0.0404	0.0404	0.0404	0.4212	0.4486	0.4

Input1	Input2	Input3	Ori	ANFIS	FIS
0.0505	0.0505	0.0505	0.4321	0.448	0.4
0.0606	0.0606	0.0606	0.4251	0.4474	0.4
0.0707	0.0707	0.0707	0.4421	0.4469	0.4
0.0808	0.0808	0.0808	0.4899	0.4465	0.4
0.0909	0.0909	0.0909	0.4548	0.4461	0.4
0.0101	0.0101	0.0101	0.4748	0.4458	0.4
0.1414	0.1414	0.1414	0.4321	0.4447	0.4
0.1818	0.1818	0.1818	0.4243,	0.444	0.4
0.2121	0.2121	0.2121	0.4889	0.4436	0.4163
0.2525	0.2525	0.2525	0.6321	0.4427	0.4397
0.2828	0.2828	0.2828	0.4521	0.4501	0.4621
0.3434	0.3434	0.3434	0.4646	0.4706	0.5163
0.3636	0.3636	0.3636	0.4436	0.4799	0.5378
0.4747	0.4747	0.4747	0.5831	0.5932	0.6801
0.4949	0.4949	0.4949	0.6321	0.6444	0.6961
0.5455	0.5455	0.5455	0.5591	0.5692	0.6795
0.5960	0.5960	0.5960	0.4999	0.5218	0.5395
0.5758	0.5758	0.5758	0.5215	0.5371	0.5821
0.6768	0.6768	0.6768	0.4652	0.4842	0.5894
0.6869	0.6869	0.6869	0.4461	0.4811	0.6116
0.7172	0.7172	0.7172	0.4142	0.473	0.6694
0.7374	0.7374	0.7374	.04651	0.4684	0.6865
0.8081	0.8081	0.8081	0.21	0.2314	0.1456
0.8283	0.8283	0.8283	0.2121	0.2222	0.1982
0.8788	0.8788	0.8788	0.1712	0.1913	0.1521
0.8990	0.8990	0.8990	0.1744	0.1744	0.1681
0.9292	0.9292	0.9292	0.1542	0.1533	0.1341

The inference system, inference rules, fuzzy inference system, rule viewer, and surface viewer for ANFIS using sugeno method is shown in appendices.

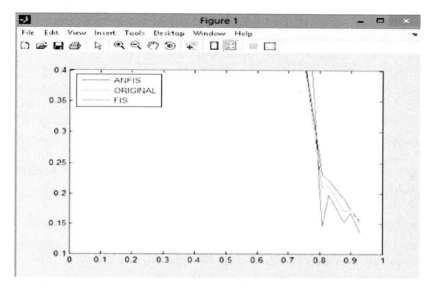

Figure 6.2   Graph of ANFIS is much close to original values than FIS

6.2.4 Results and Discussion

Experiments simulated the effect of rules with the MATLAB Fuzzy Logic Toolbox; the reliability for the values obtained was found to be very close to the calculated value. Thus, result obtained proved that approach used give accurate estimates. Results also show that the ANFIS improves the reliability evaluation of the FIS technique.

6.3 Experimental Evaluation of Optimal Service Composition within a System

TOPSIS is a well-known method for classical **multi criteria decision making** (**MCDM**) problem. These problems will usually result in uncertain, imprecise, indefinite and subjective data being present, which makes the decision-making process complex and challenging. Thus, Fuzzy TOPSIS is a method that can help in objective and systematic evaluation of alternatives on multiple criteria.

Services are core components of any SOA based application, we need service composition to answer different request. There may be a number of service compositions to get the requested task and optimal composition of these services dynamically during runtime has always been an important factor of its success. In this research, a novel idea for service composition in SOA is presented.

Service Oriented Architecture (SOA) allow service brokers to execute business processes composed of loosely coupled services offered by a multitude of service providers, and has been regarded as the main pragmatic solution for distributed environments. In such systems, each service can response the user request independently, however, many times we need service composition to answer different request and there may be a number of compositions possible to get the requested task done. Hence, it is important to find one composition which is best based on certain user preferences or criteria. This research proposes a way for selecting the optimal composition among feasible different compositions, according to certain user preferences or criteria using fuzzy TOPSIS.

To identify one among the available alternative's composition, the present research has selected the optimal composition based on several criteria like functionality closeness, integration complexity, performance, execution time, and task complexity.

6.3.1 Fuzzy technique for order performance by similarity to ideal solution – Fuzzy TOPSIS

Saghafian et.al. (2005) defined fuzzy set as: A fuzzy set ã in a universe of discourse X is characterized by a membership function $\mu\tilde{a}(x)$ that maps each element x in X to a real number in the interval [0, 1]. The function value $\mu\tilde{a}(x)$ is termed the grade of membership of x in ã. The nearer the value of $\mu\tilde{a}(x)$ to unity, the higher is the grade of membership of x in ã.

The underlying logic of TOPSIS is to define the ideal solution and negative ideal solution. The ideal solution is the solution that maximizes the benefit criteria and minimizes the cost criteria, whereas the negative ideal solution is the solution that maximizes the cost criteria and minimizes the benefit criteria (Mehdi et al. 2012). In short, the ideal solution consists of all of best values attainable of criteria, whereas the negative ideal solution is composed of all worst values attainable of criteria. The optimal alternative is the one which has the shortest distance from the ideal solution and the farthest distance from the negative ideal solution.

6.3.1.1 Linguistic Variables and Fuzzy Rating

A linguistic variable is a variable whose values are linguistic terms.

In fuzzy set theory, conversion scales are applied to transform the linguistic terms into fuzzy numbers. Linguistic terms have been found intuitively easy to use in expressing the subjectiveness and/ or qualitative imprecision of a decision maker's assessments (Zadeh 1975).

Considering the fuzziness in the decision data and group decision making process, a scale of 1 to 9 for rating the criteria and the alternatives has been used. Linguistic variables are used to assess the weights of all criteria and the ratings of each alternative with respect to each criterion, then a method to calculate the distance between two generalized fuzzy numbers is used.

6.3.1.2 The distance between fuzzy triangular numbers

Let $\tilde{a}$ = (a1, a2, a3) and $\hat{b}$ = (b1, b2, b3) be two triangular fuzzy numbers. The distance between them using the vertex method is given by:

$$d(\tilde{a}, \tilde{b}) = \sqrt{\frac{1}{3}[(a_1 - b_1)^2 + (a_2 - b_2)^2 + (a_3 - b_3)^2]}$$

(4)

The values chosen for the linguistic variables for triangular fuzzy numbers take into consideration the fuzziness and the distance among the variables. The interval chosen have a uniform representation from 1 to 9 for the fuzzy triangular numbers used for the five linguistic ratings.

6.3.2 Fuzzy TOPSIS algorithm for optimal selection

Algorithm proposed by Mehdi A.A. et al. (2012), is used for evaluating the optimal composition of services in SOA based applications. Steps are as follows:

Step 1: Set the linguistic ratings or fuzzy values for alternatives with respect to criteria.

Step 2: Weightage for each criterion is collected by decision makers.

Step 3: Evaluate all the alternatives based on the weightage of each criterion.

Step 4: Design the Fuzzy Normalized Weight Decision matrix for all alternatives.

Step 4.1: The fuzzy values $\tilde{x}_{ij}$, ($i = 1,\ldots,m; j = 1,\ldots,n$), for all the alternatives i with respect to each criteria j is chosen. And, also the appropriate fuzzy value $\tilde{w}_j$, ($j = 1,\ldots,n$) of each criteria is chosen. Here, the aggregated fuzzy rating $\tilde{x}_{ij}$ of alternative i and criteria j is calculated as shown below: $\tilde{x}_{ij} = (a_{ij}, b_{ij}, c_{ij})$

$$a_{ij} = min_k \{a_{ij}^k\};\ b_{ij} = \frac{1}{k}\Sigma_{k=1}^k b_{ij}^k\ ; c_{ij} = max_k \{c_{ij}^k\} \qquad (5)$$

Step 4.2: The aggregated fuzzy weight $\tilde{w}_j$ of each criterion is calculated as follows:

$$\tilde{w}_j^k = (w_{j1}, w_{j2}, w_{j3}) \qquad (6)$$

$$\text{where}\quad w_{j1} = min_k \{w_{jk1}\};\quad w_{j2} = \frac{1}{k}\Sigma_{k=1}^k w_{jk2}\ ;$$
$$w_{j3} = max_k \{w_{jk3}\}$$

Step 4.3: The aggregated fuzzy rating $\tilde{x}_{ij}$ of alternative i and criteria j is normalized to eliminate the anomalies. Let $\tilde{R} = [\tilde{r}_{ij}]$, ($i = 1,\ldots,m$; $j = 1,\ldots,n$) denotes the normalized fuzzy decision matrix as follows:

$$\tilde{r}_{ij} = (\frac{a_{ij}}{c_j}, \frac{b_{ij}}{c_j}, \frac{c_{ij}}{c_j})\ ; \ c_j = max_i(c_{ij}) \qquad (7)$$

Step 4.4: The weighted normalized fuzzy decision matrix $\tilde{V}$ is calculated as follows:

$$\tilde{V} = [\tilde{v}_{ij}]_{m \cdot n};\ \tilde{v}_{ij} = \tilde{r}_{ij}(.)\tilde{w}_j\ ;\quad (i = 1,\ldots,m\ ; j = 1,\ldots,n) \quad (8)$$

Step 5: Calculate $\tilde{A}max$ and $\tilde{A}max$ respectively as follows:

FPIS= $\quad \tilde{A}max = A^* = (\tilde{v}_1^*, \tilde{v}_2^*, \ldots \ldots, \tilde{v}_n^*)\ ;\qquad (9)$

where, $\quad \tilde{v}_j^* = max_i \{v_{ij3}\}\ ;\ (i = 1,\ldots,m\ ; j = 1,\ldots,n)$

FNIS= $\quad \tilde{A}max = A^- = (\tilde{v}_1^-, \tilde{v}_2^-, \ldots \ldots, \tilde{v}_n^-);\qquad (10)$

where, $\quad \tilde{v}_j^- = min_i \{v_{ij1}\}\ ;\ (i = 1,\ldots,m\ ; j = 1,\ldots,n$

Step 6: Calculate the distance between the possible alternative $v\tilde{}ij$ and the positive ideal solution distance between the weighted alternative as follows:

$$L_i^+ = \sum_{j=1}^{n} D(f, \tilde{v}_{ij}, \tilde{A}_{max}),\qquad i = 1, 2, \ldots, m,$$

$$L_i^- = \sum_{j=1}^{n} D(f, \tilde{v}_{ij}, \tilde{A}_{min}),\qquad i = 1, 2, \ldots, m. \qquad (11)$$

Step 7: Calculate the **closeness coefficient** (**CCi**) of each alternative. The closeness coefficient is calculated by taking the relative closeness to the fuzzy positive ideal solution. It is calculated as:

$$CC_i = \frac{L_i^-}{L_i^- + L_i^+} \quad L_i^- \geq 0 \quad \text{and} \quad L_i^+ \geq 0|$$

$$CC_i \in [0,1] \qquad i=1,2,3,\ldots\ldots n \qquad (12)$$

Step 8: Ranking order of all alternatives is determined, and best alternative is selected.

6.3.3 Algorithm Implementation on a Case Study

Let us assume that particular task is accomplished with the integration of several independent services executed in a particular order, this acquired task is defined in *rule engine*, which serve as a guide to an orchestration engine in the execution of the process by incorporating business rules within it.

For simplicity, we assume that to complete any task T be needs three services S1,S2,S3 available in service repository which can be combined in any order but the overall requested task efficiency may be effected for different combinations. In this case, there are six possible alternatives A1-<S1,S2,S3>, A2-<S1,S3,S2>, A3-<S2,S3,S1>, A4-<S2,S1,S3>, A5-<S3,S1,S2>, A6-<S3,S2,S1>. It assumed that the same task will also be achieved by rather different execution order of same set of services; this can be achieved dynamically by the rule engine. (*Figure 6.3*).

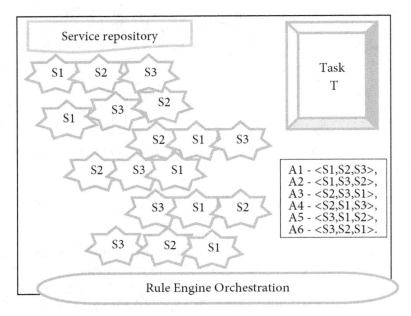

Figure 6.3 Different Feasible Service Compositions for Task T

Following are the step by step implementation of the proposed algorithm and presented on a case study to find the optimal service composition.

Step 1: Set the linguistic ratings or fuzzy values for alternatives with respect to criteria.

For simplicity and in order to understand the application of Fuzzy TOPSIS in service composition, five criteria's were taken for selection among possible alternate compositions i.e. functionality closeness, integration complexity, performance, execution time, task complexity. These criteria are taken into consideration, based on the feedback and responses taken from the industry people who are working in SOA domain. The importance of individual criteria in each possible services composition is divided into scale of 5 linguistics factors for a specific task as very low, low, medium, high and very high. Linguistic variables and fuzzy ratings for the alternatives and the criteria's are shown in *Table 6.4*.

Table 6.4   Linguistic Variables and its corresponding fuzzy rating

Fuzzy No.	Q.A Weights
$(1, 1, 3)$	VL (Very Low)
$(1, 3, 5)$	L (Low)
$(3, 5, 7)$	M (Medium)
$(5, 7, 9)$	H (High)
$(7, 9, 9)$	VH (V. High)

Step 2: Weightage for each criterion is collected by decision makers.

The ordering of services in a service composition may vary based on criteria for different task. The evaluation of best composition of services for particular task will be done with the weight matrix. Weight matrix is designed with the inputs taken from the experts or decision group. In experiment, weight matrix was designed with the input taken from five experts or decision makers. Decision makers subjective judgments develop the fuzzy criteria and use the linguistic variables (as shown in *Table 6.4*) to evaluate the ratings of alternatives with respect to each criterion as presented in *Table 6.5*.

Table 6.5   Consolidated rating for each criterion

Criteria Weightage by Decision Makers						Consolidated Rating for each Criteria	
Criteria	D1	D2	D3	D4	D5	Criteria	Rating
C1	VH	VH	H	H	VH	Functionality Closeness (C1)	VH
C2	H	H	VH	VH	M	Integration Complexity (C2)	H
C3	M	L	M	M	H	Performance (C3)	M
C4	L	M	L	VL	M	Execution time (C4)	L
C5	VL	VL	VL	L	L	Task Complexity (C5)	VL

Step 3: Evaluate all the alternatives based on the weightage of each criterion.

The above rating of decision makers for different alternative based on five different criteria is summarized and consolidated rating of each criterion is shown *Table 6.6*.

Table 6.6   Rating of 6 Alternatives by Judges under Defined Criteria's

Criteria	Alternatives	Decision Makers				
		D1	D2	D3	D4	D5
	Alternate2 (A2)	VG	G	F	VG	G
	Alternate3 (A3)	G	VG	VG	G	F
	Alternate4 (A4)	G	G	F	G	VG
	Alternate5 (A5)	P	P	G	F	F
	Alternate6 (A6)	P	P	F	VP	P
Integration Complexity (C2)	Alternate1 (A1)	F	F	P	F	VP
	Alternate2 (A2)	G	VG	F	G	VG
	Alternate3 (A3)	VG	G	VG	G	F
	Alternate4 (A4)	G	F	G	P	P
	Alternate5 (A5)	G	VP	VP	G	G
	Alternate6 (A6)	VP	P	P	F	P
Performance (C3)	Alternate1 (A1)	F	G	P	P	VP
	Alternate2 (A2)	VG	G	VG	F	G
	Alternate3 (A3)	G	VG	G	VG	G
	Alternate4 (A4)	F	P	G	G	F
	Alternate5 (A5)	P	VP	F	VP	P
	Alternate6 (A6)	F	F	P	F	F

Criteria	Alternatives	Decision Makers				
Execution time (C4)	Alternate1 (A1)	G	G	F	G	F
	Alternate2 (A2)	VG	F	G	VG	G
	Alternate3 (A3)	F	G	VG	F	VG
	Alternate4 (A4)	G	G	P	F	F
	Alternate5 (A5)	VP	P	VP	G	F
	Alternate6 (A6)	P	G	G	P	VP
Task Complexity (C5)	Alternate1 (A1)	G	F	F	VG	G
	Alternate2 (A2)	F	VG	G	G	VG
	Alternate3 (A3)	VG	G	VG	F	G
	Alternate4 (A4)	G	F	F	G	F
	Alternate5 (A5)	VP	P	VP	P	P
	Alternate6 (A6)	P	G	G	F	F

Step 4: Design the Fuzzy Normalized Weight Decision matrix for all alternatives.

The decision matrix of fuzzy ratings of possible alternatives with respect to above criteria is obtained to construct the fuzzy normalized weight decision matrix of six alternatives (shown in *Table 6.7*).

Table 6.7   Fuzzy Normalized Weight Decision Matrix of Six Alternatives (candidates)

Alternative	C1	C2	C3
A1	1.6074, 7.9486, 8.7837	2.2, 7.2413, 8.3933	1.1379, 4.9152, 6.8567
A2	6.2, 8.3256, 9.1081	5.4, 7.4721, 8.6	2.7931, 5.06591, 7.0204
A3	6.2, 7.8858, 8.8378	5.4, 6.7797, 8.083484	3, 4.6892, 6.6929
A4	5.7407, 7.1946, 8.3513	3, 6.3758, 7.8252	1.7586, 4.3502, 6.4064

Alternative	C1	C2	C3
A5	2.9851, 6.6919, 7.9729	3.4, 6.5489, 7.9801	0.7241, 4.4632, 6.4883
A6	1.6074, 7.1318, 8.2432	1.4, 6.9528, 8.2384	1.3448, 4.9152, 6.8976
Weight	6.2, 8.2, 9	5.4, 7.4, 8.6	3, 5, 7
	C4	C5	
A1	1.4, 3.4061, 5.4077	0.8518, 1.8, 3.8342	
A2	1.8, 3.3814, 5.3766	1, 1.7503, 3.7589	
A3	1.6666, 3.0593, 5.0337	1, 1.6137, 3.5945	
A4	1.1333, 2.9602, 4.9714	0.7037, 1.3862, 3.3207	
A5	0.7333, 2.9540, 4.9448	0.1851, 1.1793, 2.9783	
A6	0.8666, 3.1053, 5.1094	0.62962, 1.6758, 3.8	
Weight	1.8, 3.4, 5.4	1, 1.8, 3.8	

Step 5: Calculate $\tilde{A}max$ and $\tilde{A}min$ respectively

New simple **fuzzy positive ideal solution (FPIS)** and **fuzzy negative ideal solution (FNIS)** can be calculated by $\tilde{A}max$, $\tilde{A}min$, respectively. *Table 6.8* shows the max and min of each column of six alternatives (candidates).

Table 6.8 Max and Min of each column of six alternatives (candidates)

	C1	C2	C3
Max	8.78378, 8.8378, 9.1081	8.2384, 8.3933, 8.6	6.8567, 6.8976, 7.0204
Min	1.6074, 2.9851, 5.7407	1.4, 2.2, 3	0.7241, 1.1379, 1.3446
	C4	C5	
Max	5.1094, 5.3766, 5.4077	3.7589, 3.8, 3.8342	
Min	0.7333, 0.8666, 1.1333	0.1851, 0.6296, 0.7037	

Step 6: Calculate the distance between positive ideal solution and the weighted alternative.

The optimal alternative is the one which has the shortest distance from the ideal solution and the farthest distance from the negative ideal solution. *Table 6.9* shows the distance of each Ai (1=1,2,3,4,5,6) from A$_{max}$ and A$_{min}$.

Table 6.9 Distance of each Ai (1=1, 2, 3, 4, 5, 6) from Amax and Amin

C1

	A1	A2	A3	A4	A5	A6
Max	4.179112	1.520722	1.597373	2.043873	3.629322	4.287874
Min	3.361412	4.507516	4.270103	3.724702	2.621838	2.796298

C2

	A1	A2	A3	A4	A5	A6
Max	3.55115	1.722893	1.908483	3.271661	3.010869	4.04019
Min	4.287332	5.005174	4.575868	3.79826	3.988123	4.083732

C3

	A1	A2	A3	A4	A5	A6
Max	3.49575	2.573447	2.572812	3.30939	3.821752	3.382578
Min	3.865272	4.160259	3.932555	3.512348	3.536183	3.893926

C4

	A1	A2	A3	A4	A5	A6
Max	2.425019	2.231131	2.40567	2.698023	2.900192	2.783771
Min	2.89628	2.913644	2.639009	2.534745	2.50867	2.635641

C5

	A1	A2	A3	A4	A5	A6
Max	2.037231	1.984799	2.037027	2.267472	2.605883	2.183687
Min	1.967625	1.936878	1.824826	1.601062	1.351091	1.904324

Step 7: Calculate the closeness coefficient (CCi) of each alternative

Table 6.10   Computations of L_i^+ L_i^- and CCi

	Li+	Li	Li+ + Li	CCi	Rank
A1	15.68826	16.37792	32.06618	0.510754	4
A2	10.03299	18.52347	28.55646	0.648661	1
A3	10.52137	17.24236	27.76373	0.621039	2
A4	13.59042	15.17112	28.76154	0.527479	3
A5	15.96802	14.0059	29.97392	0.46727	6
A6	16.6781	15.31392	31.99202	0.478679	5

Step 8: Ranking order of all alternatives is determined

Finally, the values Li^+ and $Li-$ of the six possible alternatives Ai (i = 1, 2, 3, 4, 5, 6) and the closeness coefficient of each supplier is illustrated. According to the closeness coefficient, ranking the preference order of these alternatives is A2, A3, A4, A1, A6, and A5. So the best selection is alternative (candidate) A2. Therefore alternative A2 is the best choice of service composition for specific task in question considering the given criteria. The numeric values of closeness coefficient scores for alternatives can be further utilized to indicate the degree of inferiority or superiority of the alternatives w.r.t. each other.

6.3.4 Results and discussion

The fundamental part of this analysis is execution of services in an optimal way based on defined set of criteria which is found missing in most of the proposed approaches so far. The chapter discussed a numerical example and the experimental results indicate the validity and efficiency of the proposed approach. Work done in this experiments provide useful contents for those who are interested to identify services composition to support business to business or enterprise application integration in optimal way based on some defined criteria.

6.4 Experimental evaluations of performance of proposed system

Primary data was collected by visiting industry person, communicating face to face, conducting telephonic interviews and by mailing metrics designed through GQM. Secondary data for testing is collected from publication, annual reports, and records of organization under study. For the primary data, questionnaire cum personal interview method from selected managers working at these selected organizations using SOA systems is employed. Data is collected through questionnaire-cum-interview technique. Questionnaire is pre-tested on some of the managers and thus pre-tested questionnaire is then administered to all the sampled respondents. The industry people were asked to answer on five-point scale, where each point has following significance.

- Value 1 represents weak support.
- Value 2 represents minimum support.
- Value 3 represents average support.
- Value 4 represents good support.
- Value 5 represents strong support.

Factor Rating Method is used to compare traditional ERP on certain identified factors.

6.4.1 Factor Rating Method

In this method, certain factors of adoption are identified based on which, decision has to be made that whether the proposed model is efficient in comparison to traditional ERP or not. The factors were compared and analyzed on a scale of 3 in terms of difficulties that may face with the proposed model and traditional ERP systems.

- Value 1 represents Low difficulty
- Value 2 represents Moderate difficulty
- Value 3 represents High difficulty

Table 6.12 demonstrates the different factors of adoption with their score and weighted score, based on the factors and their weighted score; their graphical analysis has been done and is shown in *Figure 6.6*.

Table 6.11 Factors of Adoption

Factors	Score		Weights	Weighted Score	
	ERP	Pro-posed Model		ERP	Pro-posed Model
Security	1	2	7.0	7.0	14.0
Agility	3	1	6.5	19.5	6.5
Availability	2	1	6.5	13.0	6.5
ROI	2	1	6.0	12.0	6.0
Integration	1	1	6.0	6.0	6.0
Performance	2	2	6.0	12.0	12.0
Adaptability	2	2	5.5	11.0	11.0
Scalability	3	1	5.5	16.5	5.5
Maintainabil-ity	3	2	5.5	16.5	11.0
Migration	3	2	5.0	15.0	10.0
Mobility	3	2	5.0	15.0	10.0
Up gradation	3	1	5.0	15.0	5.0
Flexibility	3	1	5.0	15.0	5.0
Implementa-tion	3	2	4.5	13.5	9.0
Installation	3	1	4.5	13.5	4.5
Transparency	2	1	4.5	9.0	4.5
Deployment	3	2	4.0	12.0	8.0
Accessibility	2	1	4.0	8.0	4.0
Resource Competence	1	1	4.0	4.0	4.0
Total	**45**	**27**	**100**	**241.5**	**142.5**

The graph clearly shows that traditional ERP systems that have high weighted scores compared to proposed model. It has been observed during the survey that in ERP systems every factor except security has high score (only three factors i.e. integration, adaptability, and resource competence have equal score). The summation weighted scores of all factors in case of traditional ERP comes is 241.5 which is very much higher than the summed weighted score of the proposed model. This analysis clearly shows that the model is readily adaptable and much efficient than traditional ERP approach.

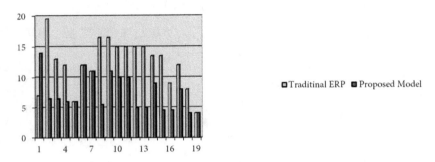

Figure 6.4   Graphical Analysis of Traditional
ERP Systems and Proposed System on Identified Factors

6.4.2 Results and Discussion

The analysis on identified factors clearly shows that model is readily adaptable and is much efficient than traditional ERP approach. It is readily deduced that traditional ERP systems involve higher levels of difficulty when analyzed in terms of agility, migration, flexibility, availability, and so on.

6.5 Evaluation of Hypothesis

A hypothesis is a tentative statement about the relationship between two or more variables. A hypothesis is a specific, testable prediction about what you expect to happen in your study. In our sample case study we take the following hypothesis to understand hypothesis evaluation and its significance.

Hypothesis:

Proposed integrated SOA model is more efficient in terms of cost and adaptability than traditional ERP systems.

T-Test method is used for the testing of Hypothesis. Using *T- Test*, we can test the hypothesis that the two independent samples come from same normal population.

6.5.1 T-Test – Analysis and Interpretation

To get the information about the ERP implementation cost, those SMEs were targeted where the IT investment cost ranges from 50 to 90 lacs. The data collected was analyzed for per user per year cost incurred by the SMEs. The cost incurred for same module if undergone by cloud of services by different companies is also analyzed. This is illustrated in *Table 6.13*.

To conduct T-test ERP utilization cost per user was evaluated and then compared with the proposed model. Total cost comprises of hardware cost, software cost, and maintenance cost (including implementation and connectivity). The total cost is then divided by the number of effective user of the application; this gives the cost per user. Sample table for calculation of per user cost is shown in *Table 6.12*.

Table 6.12 *Calculation used for 10 Companies Surveyed*

Avg software cost + Avg. hardware cost + Avg maintenance cost = Total cost	No. of effective users	Cost per user
41 + 21 + 15 = 77	53	1.45
38 + 23 + 14 = 75	57	1.31
45 + 20 + 13 = 78	49	1.59
46 + 21 + 16 = 83	50	1.66
40 + 25 + 11 = 76	65	1.16
35 + 18 + 10 = 63	75	0.84
42 + 20 + 09 = 71	52	1.36
40 + 20 + 11 = 71	90	0.78
36 + 23 + 13 = 72	56	1.28
38 + 27 + 11 = 76	55	1.38

After comparing and analyzing the two data collected for using traditional ERP and service model, it was found that cost/user/annum is much less in case of opting integrated services model.

Further t test was applied and the following results were obtained (*Table 6.13*)

Table 6.13 Hypothesis T- test

Hypothesis: Proposed Integrated SOA-Model is more efficient in terms of cost and adaptability than traditional ERP systems.					
Mean	S.D	T-test	R-t	Level of Significance (SL)	Degrees of Freedom (DF)
1.12	0.19	0.566	>1.85	5%	9
Result: Accepted					

Further to conclude, one t test is applied at 5 % level of significance using table of t-distribution for 9 degrees of freedom, we found from standard table R: t > 1.85. The calculated value for t is 0.566 which is considered within the acceptance region, and thus it can be concluded that the proposed hypothesis is accepted at 5 percent level of significance.

A large number of companies were impacted by the current economic slowdown globally. Out of total 10 companies, 6 are very much satisfied with the proposed integrated SOA architecture and have expansion plans in the near future. However, the rest of the 4 SMEs are not optimistic about a sudden change in the situation and have not planned any expansion as of now (*Table 6.14*).

Table 6.14 Company impacted by architecture

Total Respondents (%)	**Impacted by existed infrastructure**	**Expansion Plan**
60 %	Yes	Yes
40 %	Yes	No

6.5.2 Results and Discussion

Proposed hypothesis is accepted at 5 percent level of significance, and it can be concluded that the sample data indicates that proposed integrated SOA model is more efficient in terms of cost and adaptability than traditional ERP systems. Further study conducted by the research firm Gartner in the year 2010 states, adoption of integrated applications reduces cost of ownership by about 30% by lowering the software support, labor, and hardware costs. This study further supports the findings. Thus, it is concluded that proposed integrated model is ideal for medium and small sized enterprises in terms of cost benefits.

6.6 Summary

To evaluate our sample model various methods like T-Test, FIS, ANFIS, TOPSIS, and factor rating have been discussed and applied. The various factors for each sub-dimension were identified through a review of the existing literature, and discussions held with the academicians, industrial experts and consultants. On the basis of the feedback collected, a generalized model for integration of business values chain activities has been proposed. Chapter proposed three distinct soft computing techniques for evaluation of service oriented systems these are fuzzy inference system, ANFIS method and fuzzy TOPSIS. Proposed hypothesis is accepted at 5 percent level of significance and indicates that proposed integrated SOA Model is more efficient in terms of cost and adaptability than traditional ERP systems. Experience documented in this chapter will be helpful for practitioners in collecting the data necessary for reliability prediction.

Questions

Q1. List the various techniques used for analyzing service-based -systems.

Q2. You are planning to purchase a new laptop. Identify the different parameters that are important to make a final decision.

Q3. Using all parameters identified in Q2, use TOPSIS method to conclude your final decision.

Q4. Focus on some methods which are used to evaluate the reliability of any system.

Key Terms

ANFIS Adaptive Neuro Fuzzy Inference System

CMM Capability Maturity Model

CM Conceptual Model

CSF Critical Service Factors

CSS Customer Services and Support

DF   Degree of Freedom

FIS   Fuzzy Inference System

GQM   Goal Question Metric

LV   Linguistic Variables

LCIM   Level of Conceptual Interoperability Model

MCDM   Multiple Criteria Decision Making

SL   Level of Significance

TOPSIS Technique for Order Performance by Similarity to Ideal -Solution

References

- Buckley. J. (1985). "Ranking Alternatives Using Fuzzy Numbers". *Fuzzy sets and systems*. Vol. 15, No. 1, pp 21–31.

- Mehdi A.A., Nikbakhsh J., Mohammad K. (2012). "A New Fuzzy Positive and Negative Ideal Solution for Fuzzy TOPSIS". *WSEAS Transactions on Circuits and Systems*. Volume 11, No. 3, pp 48–56.

- Saghafian S., Hejazi S. (2005). "Multi-Criteria Group Decision Making Using a Modified Fuzzy Topsis Procedure". In proceedings of *Computational Intelligence for Modeling, Control and Automation*, IEEE. Vol. 2, pp. 215 –221.

- Tyagi K., Sharma A. (2012). "A Rule-Based Approach for Estimating the Reliability of Component Based Systems", in *Advances in Engineering Software*. Vol. 54, No. 2, pp 24–29.

- Wang Y.J., Lee H.S. (2007). "Generalizing TOPSIS for fuzzy multiple-criteria group decision making", *Computers and Mathematics with Applications*, Vol. 53, No. 1, pp 1762–1772.

- Zadeh L.A. (1975). "The Concept Of A Linguistic Variable And Its Application Approximate Reasoning", *Part 1, 2, and Part 3, Information -Sciences*, Vol. 8, No. 3, pp 199–249; Vol. 8, No .4, pp 301–357.